"Bays has spent years studying and wr
of Suspense. In this latest book, he t
Hitchcock's suspense techniques and
more suspenseful and how to incre
editing room."
—PETER D. MARSHALL, filmmaker, author, *Making the Magic Happen*

"Just as Jeffrey's mother forced him to watch *Rear Window* as a teen, my mother said watch *The Birds* and I'm forever thankful to both mothers for doing so. Jeffrey Michael Bays is the ultimate expert regarding Hitchcock's masterful filmmaking. Filmmakers, Hitchcock enthusiasts, film critics, and university media instructors like me need this book."
—LAURIE SCHEER, author, *The Writer's Advantage*

"*Suspense with a Camera* is the new filmmaking bible for any director who wants to gain access to Alfred Hitchcock's suspenseful bag of tricks."
—ALEX FERRARI, Indie Film Hustle

"An invaluable book for anyone looking to understand and master the fine art of filmmaking."
—STEVE LONGI, co-producer, *Hacksaw Ridge*

"The insights provided are exemplary. Bays' dissection and analysis of the Hitchcock craft should be mandatory reading for not just scholars of suspense, but for both aspiring and seasoned filmmakers hoping to hone their art by walking in the footsteps of the cinematic master."
—ADAM ROCHE, *The Secret History of Hollywood* podcast

"Bays has written a great book. He understands suspense in all the ways many people gloss over. The camera, music, photography, how to use actors, and many more ways to create suspense are here. He digs deep, we come up rich."
—DAVE WATSON, author of *Walkabout Undone*; editor, "Movies Matter"

"Bays has created a master class in suspense that is thorough, clear, and actionable. *Suspense with a Camera* is an essential read for modern filmmakers that reveals how to engage audiences through legendary director Alfred Hitchcock's classic, time-tested techniques. By investigating cinema's roots, the book serves as a powerful reminder of the wisdom that can be gained from studying the greats. It also suggests how the fundamentals of film could help chart a way forward for new forms of entertainment. There are valuable lessons here for every scholar and practitioner of film and future mediums."

—MICHAEL KOEHLER, founder, Lights Film School

"Bays' latest book deftly and confidently maneuvers between theory and craft—accomplishing the remarkable task of not only illustrating Hitchcock's techniques but giving the reader a sense of how suspense works in general as well as the tools to implement it in their own films."

—JOHN P. HESS, FilmmakerIQ

"No one knows and understands Hitchcock's train of thought better than Bays. Now that you are holding this book in your hands, walk to the front of the store and purchase this amazing resource. You will be very happy that you did."

—FORRIS DAY, JR., host, Rolling Tape

"Whether you are making a no-budget film in your backyard or a huge studio blockbuster you need to read *Suspense with a Camera* first. Filled with practical information on shots, composition, movement, and story that is required reading no matter what your genre. An advanced college film course that fits in a backpack and you can take to set every day!"

—WILLIAM C. MARTELL, writer, *Hitchcock: Mastering Suspense*

"A manifesto for manipulating audiences. Bays makes the case for the essential nature of suspense as a filmmaking device, by positing a well-researched study that walks a tightrope between academia and practicality. Bays' passion for Hitchcock and his techniques is so contagious, readers will have half a mind to set the book down and rush out to watch the entirety of Hitchcock's catalog, so they may see for themselves all that is laid out here."

—CALEB HAMMOND, *MovieMaker Magazine*

"Writers, directors, and editors of every genre can benefit from Jeffrey's clear and practical breakdown of how to craft moments of suspense."

—ANGELA BOURASSA, founder, la-screenwriter.com

SUSPENSE

WITH A CAMERA

- A FILMMAKER'S GUIDE TO -
HITCHCOCK'S TECHNIQUES

JEFFREY MICHAEL BAYS

MICHAEL WIESE PRODUCTIONS

Published by Michael Wiese Productions
12400 Ventura Blvd. #1111
Studio City, CA 91604
(818) 379-8799, (818) 986-3408 (FAX)
mw@mwp.com
www.mwp.com

Cover design by Johnny Ink. www.johnnyink.com
Interior design by William Morosi
Copyediting by David Wright
Printed by McNaughton & Gunn

Manufactured in the United States of America

Library of Congress Cataloging-in-Publication Data
Names: Bays, Jeffrey Michael, 1977- author.
Title: Suspense with the camera : A filmmaker's guide to Hitchcock's
   suspense techniques / Jeffrey Michael Bays.
Description: Studio City : Michael Wiese Productions, 2017. | Includes
   bibliographical references.
Identifiers: LCCN 2017012769 | ISBN 9781615932733
Subjects: LCSH: Hitchcock, Alfred, 1899-1980--Criticism and interpretation. |
   Suspense in motion pictures, television, etc.
Classification: LCC PN1998.3.H58 B38 2017 | DDC 791.4302/33092--dc23
LC record available at https://lccn.loc.gov/2017012769

Printed on Recycled Stock

CONTENTS

FOREWORD

BY FILM RIOT'S RYAN CONNOLLY

MY FIRST HITCHCOCK EXPERIENCE was with *Dial M for Murder* (1954) during my early teenage years when a library card was like gold to me; not because I was an avid reader, but because I discovered that you could borrow films *for free*! (Side note for anyone reading this: you still can.) Even at that age I loved classic cinema, but I was always grading on a curve considering the era in which they were made—until I discovered Hitchcock.

Dial M completely blew me away. Here was this (at that time) forty-year-old film that still managed to hold me at the edge of my seat and pull me into the story just as much, if not more, than any film I had seen in recent memory. A classic film that was remarkable by any standard. After that, just like most, I faithfully worshiped at the cinematic alter of Hitchcock.

I found a new education in film by reading about his methods, studying his films, and listening to his candid interviews. His outlook on cinema completely changed and molded how I see and approach filmmaking today. One of his biggest influences on me came from his extreme focus on crafting an experience for the audience. Hitchcock had an understanding of his audience like no one else, and a great respect for them too. That's a characteristic summed up nicely in one of my favorite quotes of his: "A good film is when the price of the dinner, the theatre admission and the babysitter were worth it."

With that focus on providing a worthwhile experience for his audience, he mastered the art of drawing us in and filling us with suspense. He prolonged tension for the audience instead of just surprising them. Hitch believed that you can turn an ordinary conversation into something fascinating just by giving your audience a single piece of information. His example was, reveal to the audience that there is a bomb under a table where the conversation is taking place. Suddenly, what was a trivial chat is now the subject of great suspense. A recent example of this exact idea in practice is during the opening scene of Quentin Tarantino's *Inglourious Basterds* (2009). A mild-tempered discussion is turned much tenser after the reveal of what's hiding below the floorboards.

From how he used his camera to how he crafted his story, the lessons of Hitchcock are invaluable and completely approachable. His genius wasn't in the expensive set pieces or locations—it was in the handling of information. It was how he would move the camera at just the right time to reveal a character's motivation, or show us a sequence of images to give us all the backstory we needed in just a few seconds. It was in the way he would make his villains charming and relatable instead of snarling monsters, or simply just let the audience know about the bomb under the table to heighten tension amidst the mundane. These are all lessons we can put into practice right now. No budget needed, just passion and whatever camera you have on you.

Of course, I'm not alone in this opinion. It's virtually impossible to dispute the indelible influence Hitchcock has had on filmmakers. With an incredible catalogue of films that have stood the test of time—from *Rebecca* (1940) to *Marnie* (1964), *The Birds* (1963), *Notorious* (1946), and my personal favorites *Rear Window* (1954), *Dial M for Murder*, *Shadow of a Doubt* (1943), *Rope* (1948), *Strangers on a Train* (1951), and of course *Psycho* (1960)—Hitchcock's incredible understanding of both the art form and his audience defined modern cinema. So many filmmakers have been deeply influenced by Hitchcock. For instance, without him we wouldn't have the same Spielberg, Scorsese, Fincher or De Palma (just to name a few).

We are all, in one way or another, made up of the masters that came before us, influencing how we create. But Hitchcock is the one nearly all of us have drawn from—and rightfully so, as he is undisputedly one of the greatest filmmakers of all time, with methods that should be studied and deciphered. Luckily for you, you are holding a solid key into unlocking much of what made him the genius he was . . . so it's time for me to shut up and let you get on with it.

—Ryan Connolly, *Film Riot*

ACKNOWLEDGMENTS

A NUMBER OF PEOPLE were invaluable in helping me complete this book.

I would like to first thank the contributors to our *Hitch20* docu-series, without whom this book wouldn't be possible: John P. Hess, William C. Martell, Forris Day, Jr., Ron Dawson, Matthew Stubstad, William Dickerson, Ben Stirek, Michael Winokur, Jordan Stone, Parker Mott, Adam Roche, Joel Gunz, Dr. Susan Smith, Jan Olsson, Leslie Coffin, Tony Lee Moral. Thanks also to those who help the series behind the scenes: Sidney Gottlieb, Ken Mogg, Dan Auiler, Chris Stone, and Dave Pattern. A big thanks to our series sponsors: Glidecam, Paralinx, Azden, Production Minds, and Michael Wiese Productions for keeping it going when times were tough. My thanks also to Zack Sharf of *IndieWire* and Kelly Leow of *MovieMaker Magazine* for the publicity, without which nobody would see the series or learn from Hitchcock's works of TV.

I'm also immensely grateful to those who have watched *Hitch20*, liked and shared it on social media, and encouraged us to continue producing the series. You inspire me with your feedback, always.

My thanks to Saar Klein, Dan Trachtenberg, William Dickerson and Paul Greengrass for providing their Q&A at the back of the book.

Much of this research would not have been possible without the La Trobe University library—such a great resource for any film scholar. Thanks to Gabrielle Murray, Anna Dzenis, and all the Cinema Studies lecturers at La Trobe University who inspired me with their wisdom while I did my Masters there.

Much appreciation to Laila Aznar for the cartoons used in chapters 14 and 20, and to Aikira Chan for the Gestalt giraffe drawing in chapter 19.

A big thanks to Michael Wiese and Ken Lee for the great books at Michael Wiese Productions, and for believing in this one. My thanks as well to fellow authors Kathy Fong Yoneda, Matt Lohr, Rona Edwards, and Laurie Scheer for your amazing support and encouragement along the way.

Eternal gratitude to my good friends Luke Zimbler, Terrell Hess, and Josiah Scott for encouraging me to continue writing Hitchcock articles and making new YouTube videos.

My love and thanks to my family for nourishing my passion for film, and letting me set sail on this journey. And of course, a special thanks to my mother for forcing me to watch *Rear Window* as a teen when I really didn't want to—an act of fate that started it all.

PERMISSIONS

The author acknowledges the copyright owners of the motion pictures from which single frames have been used in this book for purposes of commentary, criticism, and scholarship under the Fair Use Doctrine.

HOW TO USE THIS BOOK

This book is intended for a wide range of people, including:

- ◢ Aspiring filmmakers
- ◢ University film, video, or other media instructors and students
- ◢ Experienced filmmakers and screenwriters in search of clarity on "suspense making"
- ◢ Hitchcock enthusiasts seeking further appreciation of the master's works and methods
- ◢ Film critics with curiosity on what to look for in a suspense film

While the book is written to those with a script or camera in hand, hoping for guidance on how to make their current project more suspenseful, it can provide eye-opening insights to others as well. Here are some suggestions on how each group can utilize this book to the fullest:

- ◢ **Aspiring filmmakers:** If you're just starting out, you should use this book in conjunction with other books on screenwriting and directing. And it doesn't matter which genre your film fits into, it will benefit from suspense—as a way of luring the audience in and keeping them. I highly recommend *Film Directing: Shot by Shot* by Stephen Katz for his in-depth approach to shot selection and camera movement, as well as *Directing Actors* by Judith Weston for her advice on working with actors. I'm also a big fan of Robert McKee's *Story*, which is a comprehensive and lucid approach to the craft of writing for the screen, as well as *Story Is a Promise* by Bill

Johnson. It is assumed that you are already familiar with narrative terms like *protagonist* and *antagonist,* the basic three-act structure of modern scripts, and that you have a working knowledge of the differences between *plot* and *story.* We won't spend a lot of time covering story in this book, so make sure you have a solid narrative before you start.

▲ **University film, video, or other media instructors and students:** If you teach or study at a college level, this book refers to great film examples that can be viewed as a companion to the concepts covered. Throughout you'll find lists of films for suggested viewing that correspond to the topic at hand. While this is not an academic textbook, it does bridge the gap between film theory and film practice. You may find it refreshing to approach Hitchcock from a practitioner's viewpoint rather than the typical auteur theories and scopophilic analysis commonly covered in academia. This book will guide students with concepts and techniques easy to incorporate into their next project.

▲ **Experienced filmmakers and screenwriters:** Even the seasoned filmmaker can find the task of directing a suspense film a bit daunting. In the interview at the end of this book, *The Bourne Identity*'s editor Saar Klein says, "much of *Bourne* was discovered in the editing room, which led to some reshoots, re-editing and some more reshoots." It is common for films like *The Bourne Identity* to go through substantial transformations from the script to the editing phase. Tension and suspense tend to require a lot of experimentation and finesse in the editing room. With this book, you'll be able to increase your confidence early, and put emotion-based ideas into a more concrete form, and therefore find it easier to work with in scripts, storyboards, and shot lists before the edit even happens.

▲ **Hitchcock enthusiasts:** Since this book is about suspense, naturally we turn to a lot of Alfred Hitchcock's works. You'll find seeing his works from a filmmaker's perspective is an electrifying experience that will allow you to appreciate his genius that much more.

It's not uncommon for Hitchcock enthusiasts to decide to become filmmakers themselves—I certainly did. This book might be a good jumping-off point to inspire your creativity.

◢ **Film critics:** Often films are branded by their distributors as "Hitchcockian" with very little understanding of what that even means. For a critic, this book can be a useful guide to knowing what to look for in a suspense film and to having a deeper appreciation for the tricks of the trade that wind up feeling suspenseful on the screen. More importantly, this book may make it easier for you to describe why a film *doesn't* work. You may also find that my distinctions between tension, suspense, and drama will be a useful guide in writing about those weird feelings that audiences feel—without morphing them into interchangeable terms.

Even if you are none of the above, conceivably there are tricks to be learned that can translate into comic books, children's books, radio drama, presentations, theater, and even novels. While the aspects of suspense covered in this book are primarily for the movie camera, these concepts could be utilized in almost any creative endeavor.

My hope is that you will have fun and make some awesome movies!

INTRODUCTION

YOU'VE GOT A MOVIE CAMERA and you want to learn how to keep your viewers in suspense. That's what this book is for, and naturally we're going to turn to the works of the Master of Suspense for guidance. After all, when it comes right down to it, that's what director Alfred Hitchcock is famous for—making *suspense with a camera*.

When I travel around with my Hitchcock seminar, I tend to get a lot of filmmakers asking me for advice on their screenplays. There's a palpable energy and desire out there for this Hitchcockian knowledge. My hope is that this book will be a guide that you can sit down with and spend time digging up the hidden suspense in your script. Oftentimes, the solution is obvious, but you first need to get past the clichéd assumptions about suspense.

That's what this book will do. First, we'll dispel a lot of those assumptions, and then we'll step through the basic building blocks of suspense. We'll start simple and keep adding the complexities chapter by chapter. Soon you'll stumble onto "Aha!" moments that will open up your mind and spark new ways of thinking about your film project.

We'll take the flat, two-dimensional storyline of your script and activate the *audience dimension*. When you begin to acknowledge the audience, share secret information with the viewers, tease them with red herrings, and provoke them to be keenly aware of your presence as the storyteller—these all bring your story to life, off the page and off the screen.

The reason for this book is simple—you want your video, short film, or feature film to grab your audience, hold their attention, and keep them on the edge of their seats. You want them so enthralled by your story that they forget about Facebook and desperately follow every turn of the plot.

But suspense is just for the horror genre, isn't it? Not at all. Many people have a misconception or a false association between the word "suspense" and knives, blood, and screaming. One reason I wrote this book was to get beyond this cliché. I even use examples from a film you wouldn't even expect contains suspense: *You've Got Mail.* Comedies like that can have just as much suspense as *Psycho.*

Suspense for the camera is about luring the audience into a secret world and creating a close bond with the director. It's different from writing suspense for a novel, because you have the added advantage of the mobile camera. Since film is primarily a visual medium, you can move the camera toward something simple in a scene, and use the space around the actor to evoke emotion. With the camera, you can point out visual plot secrets, even those that contradict the dialogue. Once the audience is lured into these secrets, you tease them with missed opportunities, close calls, and twists. The camera creates a visual dance between storyteller and audience that allows for the audience to feel engaged on a deeper level.

I fear that a lot of really talented screenwriters and directors are missing out on key storytelling techniques because they hear "suspense" and turn their mind off to what is offered. Suspense is all about the audience's engagement with the film. All films need to engage the audience, regardless of genre.

But aren't there already a lot of Hitchcock books out there? Yes, there are many, but while their focus is on the past, mine is written purely for the modern filmmaker. While we go back and look at old films, we make them relevant to a modern context. I include examples from recent movies as well, like *The Bourne Identity, I Know What You Did Last Summer, 10 Cloverfield Lane,* and *Captain Phillips.* Be sure to read the Q&A section related to these films at the end of this book.

I do encourage you to read other Hitchcock books as resources. The interview book *Hitchcock / Truffaut* by François Truffaut is a great one, and it was certainly an inspiration for me early on. Sid Gottlieb's collections of interviews and writings from Hitchcock himself are a must read for anyone trying to learn his methods—*Hitchcock on Hitchcock* and *Alfred Hitchcock Interviews.* Dan Auiler's *Hitchcock's Notebooks* is a stunning archival resource for getting into the mind of the Master of Suspense through storyboards, production letters, and transcripts of Hitchcock's meetings with actors.

These books are all primary sources, straight from Hitchcock himself. They scratch the surface, but the whole picture is incomplete because much of what Hitchcock said to the press was for publicity rather than real advice to filmmakers. My book *How to Turn Your Boring Movie into a Hitchcock Thriller* was a fun attempt to fill in the blanks and add coherence to these archival texts.

There is also an endless number of academic texts that analyze Hitchcock through Freudian theory, motifs, tropes, and of course auteur theory. If you've ever been a film student you, no doubt, have run across some of this material.

But we need to get past all the highbrow academia and get to the true essence of how suspense is crafted for all genres. I designed this book to be an inspiration for any filmmaker out there who is ready to transform their current movie project into something ten times more compelling.

So why me?

I'm just like you—a filmmaker that wanted to learn more about creating suspense. I've been obsessed with Hitchcock for twenty years and counting. The first Hitchcock film I saw was *Rear Window* when I was fifteen. I was expecting just another boring old movie. Then as it went on I suddenly realized, "Wow, I'm really into this!" *Rear Window* seemed so real and hyper-present in the moment. This fascinated me.

How did Hitchcock do that? That question launched me on a lifelong journey to find the answers.

What started as a little checklist I wrote for myself while directing *Offing David* turned into a video, a website, and eventually grew into my docu-series *Hitch20,* an ebook, and then a traveling seminar. The more I did with this material, the more people flocked to it. There was a time that my little essays were getting three thousand readers per day, and when the videos went up, many times that. The eagerness for this material may come from modern filmmakers' need to hold viewers' attention in such a fast-paced media consumer environment.

I encourage you to watch our *Hitch20* docu-series on YouTube as a companion to this book because it includes clips from many of the examples mentioned. Many of the exciting new ideas explored here came out of that series. With *Hitch20,* our team of filmmakers and academics picked apart each of the twenty episodes of television that Hitchcock directed. We found that each episode was a goldmine of new insights into the way Hitchcock operated. Just when I thought there was nothing new to learn from Hitchcock, this series uncovered about eighty percent of the contents of this book.

So let's get started. Grab your script, shot lists, storyboards, and camera, and let's dig out the hidden suspense. I'm eager to see the great films this book inspires you to create. Email me your links to *info@borgus.com.*

—*Jeffrey Michael Bays (October 2017)*

PART ONE:
DIGGING UP THE SUSPENSE

CHAPTER 1
SUSPENSE

STORY ISN'T ENOUGH.

With so much competition out there today, and an omnipresent land-scape of media outlets, filmmakers worry about one thing: *How do I keep viewers (if they actually manage to start watching) engaged in my material?*

The answer everyone falls back on is *story*. Most speculate that if you can just come up with a compelling story, then viewers will all be on board with your film. But the simple fact is, you have to have more than a good story to keep your audience.

Suspense has nothing to do with blood and knives and women scream-ing. Instead, it's that thing that keeps viewers hanging on to see the outcome of your movie. It's about connecting with your audience, mak-ing them care, making them so involved in your story that they can't turn away.

Even if your creative project is a comedy skit, a music video, a sci-fi fea-ture film, or a romantic comedy for the Hallmark Channel—you need suspense. Every story you do for an audience needs suspense.

There once was a large British man who was really good at suspense. In fact, to date, he is still the best there ever was. It has been a half cen-tury since his last film was released, yet we're still able to learn from him. We're still finding out new tricks from his work. When I give talks to groups of screenwriters and filmmakers, I see them light up when I mention this historic film legend.

Yes, I'm talking about Alfred Hitchcock. Most people call him Hitch for short. You'll be hearing a lot about him in this book.

All ages seem to love Hitch, whether it be the millennial film enthusiast studying film in college, or the baby boomer that remembers growing up with his TV show as a kid.

Most all of his works of film and television still hold up today for one reason: suspense. Suspense transcends time and era, and captures that raw universal human nature in all of us. Once you learn how to use it, you'll never look at storytelling quite the same again.

LURING THE AUDIENCE AND KEEPING THEM

Before getting the audience to feel suspense, you have to start by luring them in and keeping them. I have boiled this down to three key elements that all films must have in order to resonate with an audience. As a director setting sail on your new project, these are the three primary things you must consider: *mood, momentum,* and *manipulation.*

MOOD

Firstly, a good film captures and delivers a mood, or a series of moods. As you may have read in my book *Between the Scenes*, shifting moods gives the audience a satisfying emotional change as a film progresses.

It occurs to me that a great deal of film students and amateur filmmakers are driven to make films of their own because they're chasing after something—a vague feeling or aesthetic—that they enjoyed in their favorite movies. Fan fiction, after all, is about recapturing the essence of a film you liked, say, about *Star Wars* or any classic film noir.

There's something romantic about re-creating that feeling you get when a detective in a fedora hat walks down a dark alley with a cigarette. You hear a voice-over with a sarcastic macho voice telling you about how his days of crime fighting are giving him the blues. That's not story! But that mood-setting effect has a profound impact on us. We're already hooked.

Recent psychological studies have demonstrated that when we sit down and watch a movie, our emotional state changes to emulate what's on the screen. So yes, mood is a huge factor to consider when designing your film. Your job as a storyteller is, first, to be a mood setter.

MOMENTUM

Once you've established a mood, you must propel things forward and generate momentum. You may assume this means story, but that's not the only way to get things moving forward.

Nobody ever gets onto a roller coaster and asks, "OK, what's the story?" Of course not. There is no story on a roller coaster, but this doesn't stop us from enjoying the ride, being jostled around safely at high speeds and letting gravity pull us forward.

In movies, momentum—that forward feeling of anticipation—is generated by various things. Here are some:

◢ Hitchcock was able to use glances and subjective camera language to lure you into a character's hidden secretive world.

◢ Sexual attraction is another one—if an alluring actor is on the screen, we have a tendency to hang on to see what they do, in fascination.

◢ There's also the rubbernecking effect—the thing that causes people to slow down and gawk when they see an accident on the side of the road.

◢ Comedy is another one. If someone makes us laugh, we wait to see what clever hijinks they'll come up with next.

◢ When a character is faced with a universally understood situation, we immediately form empathy, and wait to see how they handle it.

Creating that kinetic, forward-moving momentum keeps your audience interested in what's coming next. They'll hang on to find the beginnings of story, and get carried along for the ride.

MANIPULATION

Card tricks and magic acts work because we enjoy the art of trickery. Audiences love being fooled! Moviemakers, too, must grasp this art and make it their ultimate goal. You must manipulate your audience's expectations. Use red herrings, proverbial trap doors, mirrors, sleights of hand, and other gags to get your audience to think, "I've been tricked, and I like it!"

First manipulate what they know, and provoke them into wondering about what they don't know. Give your audience secret information that the characters don't know, let one character withhold a secret from another, or mislead the audience with false information. Then, by cleverly revealing this secret in a dramatic way, you create a sense of satisfaction in the audience.

As a director you must play with the basic psychological need for closure—that compelling itch to solve a puzzle. Just one more move and it will be solved. The audience—like a mouse—when trapped in a compelling mental maze, must feel like they're on the cusp of the exit. But then, you have to give them a surprising new way out before they reach that exit. They will love the feeling that they've discovered a secret door or a cheat code to get past the expected outcome.

Audiences want to be playfully manipulated and tricked. They need to feel that the movie isn't just meandering randomly, that the events aren't just happening "because." Audiences need the satisfaction that someone has an intelligent plan, that there's something profound to be learned from these events, and that the director has found a way to outwit our skepticism and make us feel it unexpectedly. If your film doesn't manipulate, no amount of story is going to compensate.

WHAT IS SUSPENSE?

That brings us to suspense. Suspense combines those basic elements of mood, momentum, and manipulation and sets up gripping situations that make audiences squirm.

Surprisingly, the exact way cinematic suspense works has been difficult to pinpoint. Saar Klein, editor of *The Bourne Identity*, says, "building suspense is an intuitive process that is hard to verbalize." Dan Trachtenberg, director of *10 Cloverfield Lane*, says it's difficult to tell when suspense is working during production. "When you're making one of these movies none of it is scary or suspenseful while you're shooting nor editing." (See our interviews in Part Seven.)

American film scholar Noël Carroll, along with cognitive psychologists, has long believed that suspense is dependent on a feeling of "uncertainty" about the outcome of events. Film scholar Aaron Smuts seems to have debunked the whole idea, proving that uncertainty really isn't a part of it at all. He and film scholar David Bordwell became skeptical while trying to solve the Paradox of Suspense by examining the fact that repeated viewings don't have a diminished effect on the feelings of suspense. In some instances suspense even increases the second time a film is watched. The motel office scene in *Psycho* (1960), for instance, between Marion Crane and Norman Bates becomes much more suspenseful for those who have already seen the film and know the outcome (Smuts).

But Bordwell postulates that suspense is more of an instinctual reflex in our autonomic systems—that because suspense calls upon emotional instinct rather than our higher reasoning, we experience it the same each time regardless of plot spoilers. So rather than being uncertain about an outcome, we simply get a tickle of the funny bone each time we are exposed to a suspenseful scene.

Perhaps that explains why football fans can record a game and then watch parts of it over again later. It would seem that certain unique moments of a game are enjoyed on repeat viewings simply because of their uniqueness, not based on knowledge of the final score. The fact that these unique moments will never occur again in future games in quite the same way makes them special enough to watch over and over again.

So if it's not about uncertainty, then what is it about? Aaron Smuts says there's more to it, that suspense is actually a *frustration* in the viewer, frustration that we can't change the outcome. We can't step in and help when things are going down the wrong path. Back to football—all you can do is cheer or yell at the TV.

This explains why the most suspenseful Hitchcock scenes are moments where no one helps, and the audience is reminded that they are also unable to help. We're forced to watch and wait—in suspense.

▲ A nearby policeman doesn't try to rescue Alice while she's being raped in *Blackmail* (1929).

▲ We can't stop the brakeless car from speeding down the winding hill in *Family Plot* (1976).

▲ We can't help Bruno pick up the lighter he's dropped down the storm drain in *Strangers on a Train* (1951).

That last one is especially interesting, because we feel suspense even when the antagonist (the bad guy) needs help succeeding. Hitchcock was able to call upon our rescue instinct and create situations where we are helpless to intervene. This feeling of frustration is a big part of suspense, and of our enjoyment of it. Somehow it's entertaining for us to have these feelings provoked while watching a movie.

So, in essence, suspense is about provoking that *rescue instinct* in all of us. When we see someone stepping in front of a bus, or a child chasing a ball in front of a car, or a dog trapped in a river—we want to reach out and save them.

I take this a step further in my docu-series *Hitch20*, saying that the key to suspense is to set up secrets within the story that mustn't be found out by the other characters. Pitting these characters against each other on the cusp of revealing the secret—that's where we get suspense. I'll have more things to add to this definition of suspense as we go on. But first, a word about the difference between tension, drama, and suspense.

TENSION & DRAMA VS. SUSPENSE

If that script you're writing or film you're producing already has a lot of tension and drama, maybe it's still missing suspense. There are important differences between tension, drama, and suspense. At this point, we need to make sure we delineate the difference between them, because they are often used interchangeably and this can get confusing.

Let's pretend you're on a phone call with a close friend.

Tension is if there's static on the line, or there's something abnormal going on that requires you to work extra hard to focus on the conversation.

Drama is if your friend is telling you juicy gossip or getting upset with you about something.

Suspense is when your friend suddenly stops talking in mid-sentence. Did she hang up? Did something happen to her? Will she call back? That's suspense. It provokes a lot of questions that keep you wondering if and when this will be resolved.

TENSION

Tension is smaller and more immediate than suspense. To understand the distinction between the two, imagine a slingshot being pulled back tight, aimed right at your face. Tension is the tightness of the rubber band. Suspense is that nagging question: "Is he really going to let go? Or, when is he going to let go?"

Another way to look at the difference is with a tightrope walker. Imagine the long rope stretched tight, creating enough tension to keep the walker secured and balanced. As he walks toward the middle and begins to wobble, suspense is that perpetual question: "Is he going to fall?"

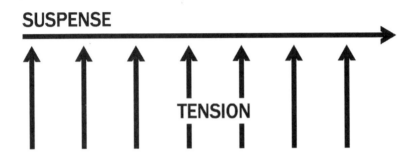

Figure 1.1. Suspense is an overall question about the outcome made up of smaller moments of tension.

But, again, it's not that uncertainty that generates suspense. Instead, it's the fact that we can't reach in and catch him before he falls. It makes our muscles freeze; our breath stops and we wait with our mouths open to see what happens.

In a film, tension (fig. 1.1) is the moment-by-moment feeling of intensity created by the audiovisual artifice. Tension is created by the shot selection, the editing rhythm, the music, the sounds, and every other artistic element that goes into a scene to make it feel bold and tactile. Tension is synthesized and imposed onto the narrative through the choice of camera placement/movement and editing. Constricting space and time in the shots and pacing of the edits can increase tension. See chapters 6 and 14 for more about this.

DRAMA

Drama is different from suspense and tension because it is an emotion that derives from conflict between characters and environment.

You could say drama is a form of tension as well, but we need to easily demarcate it for the purposes of this discussion. Drama is made from dialogue beats, character conflict, and all of those narrative elements that we are used to learning in film school.

Drama is generated through the narrative. When the actors debate with dialogue, this takes on the drama of the stage, relieved by plot revelation, scene changes, and surprise twists. Dramatic tension is increased when the approach of the desired relief is delayed or complicated by plot points or antagonistic forces.

Constricting space and time in the environment surrounding the actors—for example, a ticking clock counting down to an explosion—is a narrative device used to increase drama. That's not automatically suspense, but you can turn that ticking clock into suspense in the way it's treated. More on that later.

Tension, drama and suspense are easy to confuse because they are all similar feelings and they do work together. They are all present at different times throughout a good movie. For the most part, in this book we'll be focusing primarily on suspense and tension. Drama is something for other books to tackle.

FRAMEWORK OF CREATING SUSPENSE

Suspense won't work without audience empathy. Creating empathy for the protagonist (the good guy) is key to feeling suspense, especially when there is an anticipation of danger. We feel a desire to see the hero get to safety because we already have an emotional connection with the hero, or we relate to her dilemma on some basic universal level.

The first step in engaging this empathy is *not* simply to throw the protagonist into a scary situation. Instead, it's about luring the audience with secret information.

Here are the basic steps for creating suspense in your film:

1. Plant secrets
2. Build close calls
3. Sleight of hand

Suspense in film is about planting a secret within your story-world, and then building in some close-call moments to tease the audience about that secret getting out. At the end of the suspense sequence, which may be a short scene or span across an entire film, you'll want to pull a magician's sleight of hand in a surprise twist.

That ticking bomb scenario only becomes suspense if someone doesn't know about it. If everyone in the film knows about the timer and is just racing quickly to beat it—that's not suspense. The distinction is in whether the bomb itself is a secret that must be discovered before it's too late.

STEP 1: START PLANTING SECRETS

In order to start constructing a framework for suspense in your film, you must first have a hidden secret. Person A is hiding something. This secret is an essential piece of information in your story that you use to manipulate the audience.

First, reveal the secret to the audience, and then create a moment with another character from whom the secret must be concealed.

The most basic form of this is: Person A lies to Person B.

A lie primes the audience. Once the lie is told to another character it immediately piques our attention. We think, "Oh, she just lied to him!" This calls upon our basic human instincts to make judgments about both the person lying and the person being lied to. It sets up an open chasm in your storytelling ride that demands closure.

Most importantly, the secret knowledge makes the audience feel special, that they have been given access to this secret that no one else knows. This activates that basic human pleasure of receiving gossip.

In the above example, when the lie is told to Person B, a bond is formed between the audience and Person A.

And Person A doesn't have to be the protagonist either. In Hitchcock's *Lifeboat* (1944), for example, the antagonist, a German captain, lies about a lot of things. He lies about having a compass, lies about having extra water, lies about the course they should take. Through special obvious camera moves onto his compass, watching him secretly drinking water, etc., Hitchcock shows us these secrets before the captain lies about them. We also get increased enjoyment through the captain's poker-faced grin. These are secrets that only we know about, and if they get out could shift the entire plot in another direction.

As the audience, we suspect that the captain in *Lifeboat* is planning to lead the protagonists into enemy territory, but we still have some faith that he'll do the right thing. Each time he lies, it engages the curiosity of the audience.

STEP 2: CLOSE CALLS

Once the audience is lured into a secret, it's time for this secret to get out (fig. 1.2). That is, of course, something that the audience doesn't want to happen, but simultaneously wishes to happen. There is a kind of special dual enjoyment the audience experiences teetering between sympathy and schadenfreude (enjoyment of others' pain).

And it's the job of the suspense director to build scenarios that tease with missed opportunities and close calls, to dance on the head of that pin of chance. You want your audience to squirm, hoping things will succeed yet wanting to see explosions of drama.

Close-call moments are the key to suspense and activating our frustrated rescue instinct. As Bordwell said, in the moment of suspense our autonomic nervous system is activated. In a way, we feel a close-call moment as a live event happening in real time.

In *I, Confess* (1953) an innocent priest is on trial for murder. He knows who the real killer is and could reveal it at any time to save his own hide. But the priest must protect this secret because it was revealed to him in the confessional box. By the time we get to the trial, Hitchcock has built up such momentum around this secret that we desperately want the priest to spill the beans during the trial and save himself. The scene is filled with nervous reaction shots of the killer, anticipating exposure at any moment. It never happens, and the close call is thwarted, for now.

Figure 1.2. A character with a secret hides the secret from other characters. Suspense is heightened as the secret gets closer and closer to exposure.

By creating entertaining scenes that set up delicious opportunities for the secret to be exposed, you heighten the suspense.

Going back to the tightrope analogy, a man is balancing on a high wire and the suspense question is: Will he fall? The next thing you want to do as the storyteller is to begin to answer this question but withhold the answer at the last minute, thus teasing the audience.

The man begins to wobble and he struggles to keep his balance on the high wire. The question "Will he fall?" is provoked and intensified as the man wobbles further. Within moments, the man recovers his balance. Boy, that was close!

A "that was close!" moment is essential in increasing suspense. It kept that nagging fear alive, plus it gave the audience the enjoyment of a near-miss.

In the gambling world, there's a thing psychologists have discovered where a gambler will become addicted after an almost-win (Reid). When three lemons come up on the slot machine, but not the winning fourth, the player perceives this almost-win as a lucky streak. He continues playing even more intently, believing that he is closer to winning on the next round. This near-miss effect leads to gambling addiction. Neurologists have been able to determine that the reward center of the brain is activated almost as much on an almost-win as with an actual win.

Translating this psychology into the moviegoing world, when there's a close call in a suspense situation, it gives the audience the thrill of closure without actually providing closure. The viewer becomes addicted to hanging on to see if the next "that was close!" moment will actually result in real closure.

In the example earlier, when Person A lies to Person B, this is a close-call moment. There's a chance that Person B will catch on and discover the secret being withheld. The suspense director will milk this moment for all it's worth, in an elaborate and playful tease. This keeps the momentum going until the next close call.

Jonah Lehrer of *Wired Magazine* gives a fascinating analysis of this teasing effect in relation to our enjoyment of music. He says that good music works because it flirts with our expectations of order, denying its own form and provoking us to anticipate closure. Here's how Lehrer explains it:

> *Before a musical pattern can be desired by the brain, it must play hard to get. Music only excites us when it makes our auditory cortex struggle to uncover its order. If the music is too obvious, if its patterns are always present, it is annoyingly boring. This is why composers introduce the tonic note at the beginning of the song and then studiously avoid it until the end. The longer we are denied the pattern we expect, the greater the emotional release when the pattern returns, safe and sound.* (Wired 2010)

That's a lot like how good suspense works in the movies, too. The film suggests a pattern of events that play "hard to get," teasing us with close calls, yet denying closure. The longer we are denied the closure we expect, the greater the release when it finally resolves.

STEP 3: SLEIGHT OF HAND

Creating suspense isn't fun for the viewer unless it's resolved and real closure is provided. Once the suspense has been maximized in your film, you actually should provide closure to reward the audience for hanging on for so long. Otherwise the suspense will be wasted and they probably won't want to watch the film again.

Closure should never turn out the way that's expected. The surprise twist is the best way to satisfy this closure, just like a magician's sleight of hand.

A magician makes you think he has put the coin into his left hand, even though it is still in his right hand. He pays so much attention to the empty left hand that he convinces you that the coin is there. During this distraction, his right hand can do nearly anything unnoticed. Even the most hard-nosed skeptic will be surprised when the magician opens his left hand to reveal it is empty, and then opens his right hand to reveal the coin.

Magic works because audiences love being fooled. They know this going in. There is an unspoken agreement between audience and magician that he will fool them. The pleasure his audience members gain from this comes through the clever ways the magician will outwit their skepticism. He uses showmanship, red herrings, and fear to manipulate the moment-to-moment expectations of the human mind.

When it comes right down to it, suspense is a form of trickery. When a magician fools you with sleight of hand, you tend to giggle. Even if you know there's some trick, you're still impressed that he was able to pull it off in front of your eyes without you noticing. That feeling of surprise when you find out you've been fooled—that's classic storytelling.

So in the previous example, the tightrope walker wobbles and begins to fall. It looks like it's all over for him. At the last minute the camera reveals that this entire time the rope has only been two feet off the ground. He stumbles onto the ground unharmed. We get a simultaneous sigh of relief and a chuckle because we've been fooled.

Just like a magician has to work hard to get his tricks to work flawlessly, a filmmaker can learn the craft of increasing suspense in their creative works and paying it off with a surprising twist.

WHAT SUSPENSE IS NOT

Amateurs (and probably a lot of professionals) mistakenly think that suspense is a result of teasing upcoming information—that if you keep information just out of reach of the viewer, like a carrot on a stick, they'll hang on long enough to find out some juicy plot information that will solve the puzzle.

There is some merit in this form of storytelling. *2001: A Space Odyssey* does it beautifully. The mystery and lack of information in *2001* keeps you intrigued enough to wait patiently for the next clue to appear. But that's not suspense.

Suspense, at least the Hitchcockian kind, requires that the audience knows as much information as the characters do, if not more so. When the audience knows more than the characters do, it creates an entertaining frustration that they can't affect the outcome.

Take these two examples and decide which one is more suspenseful:

Example 1: A toddler has just learned to walk and his parents have put him on a moving treadmill as a joke. The child gleefully steps along at the right pace to stay on. Then he gets a little too brave and walks backwards. This slows him down and he nearly falls off the bottom edge of the treadmill. Just at the last minute he spins back around and walks quickly to catch up.

Example 2: A woman creeps up a dark staircase. Her feet softly and elegantly step, her trembling hand steadies herself on the railing. If only she had a flashlight, she could see. A wolf howls in the distance. She continues to climb until she gets to the top of the stairs and slowly peers around the corner.

Now, I think a lot of people would buy into all the dark imagery of Example 2 and believe that it was the more suspenseful of the two. Most likely, however, the audience is going to be more invested in the toddler in Example 1. Why?

First of all, we know nothing about the woman. There's no story, no empathy, and nothing is revealed. She's walking into a dark unknown. It's a very flat, meaningless exercise of synthetic tension but does nothing to tell us why we should care.

The toddler, on the other hand, has an obvious close call. We know his parents have set him up on this treadmill, and that it probably isn't a good idea. Even though he is successful at walking on the treadmill, there is a "that was close!" moment. He almost falls off, and most likely could have gotten injured. We are relieved when he doesn't fall, but he could still fall at any moment. His safety is uncertain.

The woman's safety is uncertain, too, but we don't know what the danger is. It's just a vague mood set by howling wolves, dark lighting, and weird noises. Is a ghost going to grab her? Will a serial killer pop out with a knife? Is she delusional? Until we find out more, there's no real suspense. This is mood setting in place of suspense building.

Notice that the toddler scene makes no mention of lighting. There are no wolves or shadows. The suspense is there because of the situation, in spite of the mood.

In order to build real suspense into the staircase scenario, you'd want to show the audience what's around the corner. Plant the seed of a real threat that is unbeknownst to the woman. Then have the woman nonchalantly walk up the stairs without a care in the world. This now becomes the classic stairway scene from Jim Gillespie's *I Know What You Did Last Summer* (1997). The audience knows the killer is upstairs and Helen doesn't have a clue he's even in the house. She walks right toward him!

Now you have suspense, because the audience knows more than Helen does, and wants to warn her. But we can't help. We can't jump through the screen and save her. All we can do is watch with our jaws open, waiting helplessly in anticipation.

To sum it up: You want to plant a secret within your story-world, and then build in some "that was close!" moments to tease the audience about that secret getting out. After a few of those close calls and heightened suspense, you'll want to resolve it with a sleight-of-hand—a surprise twist that leaves the audience amused that the expected outcome didn't occur.

In the next chapter we'll explore further ways to plant secrets within your film, to bring out the audience's feeling of engagement.

SUGGESTED VIEWING

▲ *Lifeboat* (1944)

▲ *I, Confess* (1953)

FURTHER READING

Auiler, Dan 2001. *Hitchcock's Notebooks: An Authorized and Illustrated Look Inside the Creative Mind of Alfred Hitchcock*, Harper Collins, New York.

Bays, Jeffrey 2015. "Filmmakers: Does Story Really Matter?" *Medium.com* blog.

Bordwell, David 2007. "This Is Your Brain on Movies, Maybe," David Bordwell's Website on Cinema, *www.davidbordwell.net*.

Cleland, Jane 2016. *Mastering Suspense, Structure & Plot*, F+W Media, Ohio.

Lehrer, Jonah 2010. "The Science of Eavesdropping," *Wired* (9/10/10).

Reid, R. L. 1986. "The Psychology of the Near Miss," *Journal of Gambling Behaviour*, 2 , 32–39. University of Exeter, England.

Schickel, Richard 1973. *The Men Who Made the Movies: Hitchcock*, The American Cinematheque TV series.

Smuts, Aaron, "The Paradox of Suspense," *The Stanford Encyclopedia of Philosophy* (Fall 2009 Edition), Edward N. Zalta (ed.), URL = <*https://plato.stanford.edu/archives/fall2009/entries/paradox-suspense/*>.

Wulff, Hans J. & Jenzowsky, Stefan 2000. "Suspense/Tension Research of the Film," *Medienwissenschaft: Rezensionen* (13,1, 1996, pp. 12–21).

SUSPENSE MYTH NO. 1

**I WANT SUSPENSE, SO MY LIGHTING SCHEME
SHOULD BE DARK**

False. Hitchcock proved many times over that suspense can be achieved (and even heightened) in bright, sunny atmospheres. Just look at the crop duster scene in *North by Northwest*, where he staged an attempted murder in an empty farm field in mid-afternoon.

He was also an advocate of comic openings for drama. By starting your film with playful music and a comic mood, you warm up your audience and win their affection. Once the audience is laughing and bonding with your characters, you start to introduce the drama. This drama has more impact because it contrasts so starkly with the comedy, and your audience is now invested in the characters' outcome.

Starting dark and creepy may create a sense of curiosity and mystery, but the on-the-nose obviousness of it all will likely leave your audience yawning. ◢

CHAPTER 2
THE TRIAD OF SECRETS

BY THIS POINT, you may be catching on to the ideas behind creating suspense, but it might still be too intimidating to start diving into your script to make changes.

First, a reminder of our goal from the previous chapter: You want to plant a secret within your story-world, and then build in some "that was close!" moments to tease the audience about that secret getting out. After a few of those close calls and heightened suspense, you'll want to resolve it with a sleight-of-hand—a surprise twist that leaves the audience amused that the expected outcome didn't occur.

Planting that secret is what we'll focus on now. In order to construct a suspense sequence, you first need to have a secret planted within either the protagonist, audience, other characters, or a combination of the three. Let's call it the Triad of Secrets. The most important part of the triad is the audience.

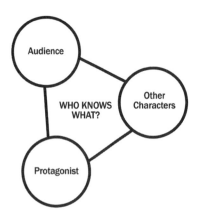

Figure 2.1. Triad of Secrets – Determining who knows secrets among the audience, protagonist, and other characters is the key to creating close calls and building suspense.

Imagine we're in a classroom and I choose someone from the audience to leave the room for a few minutes. While he's gone, I reveal an important secret to everyone that he misses out on. I tell everyone that when the man comes back I'm going to give him fifty dollars in cash if he touches his nose, but I'm not going to warn him in advance.

Then he comes back in the room, and I invite him up on stage. He knows nothing about the nose gag or the fifty dollars, so I tease the audience by trying different ways to coax him into accidentally touching his nose. The audience giggles. I engage him in random conversation, letting him fidget around uncomfortably. The audience intently watches his confused reaction and giggles even more.

At one point, he randomly scratches his ear and the audience gasps. So close! The poor guy doesn't know what's going on.

In this scenario we've created an interesting dynamic where the audience has been lured into taking sides. They become intently invested in my goal of provoking a nose-touch, and the innocent man's ignorance of what's happening makes it so much fun.

This is the very basic concept of creating suspense.

To build suspense in your screenplay, movie, or short film (any storytelling mode, really), you need to plant secrets within your story-world and then create a nagging question surrounding whether those secrets are going to get out.

Start by surveying the plot information in your story between three groups of people—the Triad of Secrets (fig. 2.1).

Here's what you need to figure out:

1. What does the protagonist know?
2. What do the other characters know?
3. What does the audience know?

If they all know the same things, you may have a problem. If that guy on stage knew about the fifty dollars, no suspense. If the audience didn't know about the fifty dollars, still no suspense.

In the Triad of Secrets, a filmmaker must play a game with plot secrets between the protagonist, the audience, and the other characters. Each of these three parts of the triad are going to hold different access to plot secrets. It is then pitting these levels of access against each other that creates suspense.

PROTAGONIST'S SECRETS

If you have a script that you're working on right now, or a movie in production, think about the plot information that the protagonist knows and when they know it. Do they hide that information from other characters? What will happen to the protagonist if that information gets out?

Probably the easiest example of this is the 1950s TV series *Leave It to Beaver.* The young kid, Theodore Cleaver, is always getting himself into trouble. He does something wrong and must hide it from his parents, because he fears his dad will "yell" at him. Much of the fun of this series is watching Beaver—and often his friend Larry—sneaking through the kitchen to avoid getting caught.

Moments like these, where the secret almost gets out, are ripe for suspense. A fun moment like this can be played for laughs right along with the tension. In fact, you can use the ignorance of the supporting characters for comic effect, and thus raise tension with a comedic close call.

What kind of secrets can be hidden by the protagonist? Here are some common movie examples of hidden secrets that generate suspense:

- ◢ Got fired from job, hiding it
- ◢ Hiding a birthday gift and/or planning surprise party
- ◢ Sneaking into an unauthorized place

◢ Did something illegal or plans to in future
◢ Hidden identity or important aspect of past
◢ Bought expensive item without permission of spouse/parent
◢ Engaged or pregnant, hiding it from parents
◢ Hiding lottery winnings and/or found treasure
◢ An affair

Secrets like these call upon our basic emotions, something that we have all experienced, especially in childhood. The fear of getting caught is a universal fear that crosses through all cultures and all ages. It goes back to our ancestral humans on the savanna hiding from that nearby lion getting a whiff of human scent. It's primal, and that's why it works so well in movies.

> *People always enjoy seeing someone doing something without being discovered, as to whatever form it takes. Even if you have a villain creeping in, the audience for some reason, whether there's a touch of larceny in everyone or something, I don't know, will always say "Quick, quick, before you're found out. Get out, get out."*—ALFRED HITCHCOCK (Auiler)

Calling upon those instinctual fears of getting caught grabs the audience's empathy and brings them to the side of the character. Regardless of what crime they've done, or the severity of the secret being hidden, we tend to side with them for the enjoyment of the narrative. We want to see how it plays out. We want to see the cave man escape the lion.

It's a "that was close!" moment.

For a great contemporary example of this, see the first episode of HBO's *The Night Of* (2016). Protagonist Nasir (Riz Ahmed) wakes up in a strange woman's house and realizes that she has been murdered. Fearing that he would be blamed, he grabs the bloody knife and drives away. When the cops pull him over for reckless driving, they arrest him only for being intoxicated. The cops are then called to the crime scene to investigate, unaware that Nasir is connected. He must sit in the police car as the crime is discovered in front of him, and then sit in the police station hoping no one sees the knife in his coat pocket.

The episode is full of suspense as we fear that he'll get caught. It's an excellent example of using a secret to full advantage.

AUDIENCE'S SECRETS

Now what does the audience know? Does the audience know the same information at the same time that the protagonist does? Does the audience know more than the protagonist knows? Less?

When we see a character lying, we notice it right away. We feel privileged in the secret knowledge that we have within the story's world. It immediately causes us to internalize the information being lied about.

In Hitchcockian suspense, the audience should know plot secrets before the characters. This way, the characters' ignorance make us want to jump onto the screen and help warn them: "Don't go around that corner!"

> Let the audience play God ... If the audience has been told all the secrets that the characters do not know, they'll work [really hard] for you because they know what fate is facing the poor actors. That is what's known as "playing God." That is suspense.—ALFRED HITCHCOCK (Gottlieb)

Hitchcock referred to this audience-centric advantage as the Bomb Theory.

In the Bomb Theory, the viewer is given secret information that the characters don't know. For example: There's a bomb under the table. When the clueless characters sit around the table laughing and gossiping about something entirely trivial, we want to warn them about the bomb. But of course, we can't. That gives us excruciating suspense (Schickel).

That's why movies about investigations like director Tom McCarthy's *Spotlight* (2015) are not purely suspense. They keep you waiting until the last scene to solve the case. Sure, there is a level of curiosity about solving the crime and following the journalists on their pursuit of evidence and interviews. Naturally, the antagonists know everything and are keeping it secret. They may be elusive, clever, or even threatening, making things dramatically interesting. That's not enough for suspense, *unless* the audience is clued in on the secrets before the journalists are. That way you can build suspense around whether the antagonists will be able to maintain the secret.

Now, an important distinction should be made here. There are varying degrees of knowledge that the audience can have. It's not always knowledge of one hundred percent of the secret at first, and that secret can grow and change. In *Torn Curtain* (1966), Hitchcock creates suspense out of a press conference. The opening act surrounds a secret that Michael is keeping from his fiancée, Sarah. The audience knows full well that there is a secret, but we're just not sure what the secret is. Hitchcock shows us the secret telegram, the secret code within the book, and we know that it's really important for Michael to hide it from Sarah. We just don't know what it is until, thirty minutes into the film, he holds a press conference and we find out right along with Sarah in real time. The most suspenseful press conference ever!

But in *Torn Curtain*, that press conference didn't reveal one hundred percent of the secret. In fact, it turned out to be a ruse to hide another, deeper secret, which carries the suspense for yet another thirty minutes.

Hitchcock believed that giving the audience knowledge of the secrets greatly affects the second viewing of the film, and whether the suspense will be as effective the next time around. Here's what he said:

> *I'm a great believer in making sure that if people see the film a second time they don't feel cheated. That is a must. You must be honest about it and not merely keep things away from the audience. I'd call that cheating. You should never do that.*—ALFRED HITCHCOCK (Gottlieb)

Director Paul Greengrass's opening sequences of *Captain Phillips* (2013) spend an equal amount of time following both the protagonist and antagonist. As the audience, we know well in advance that these Somali pirates are planning to attack the cargo ship. The closer they get, the more suspense builds. Then, once the protagonist realizes they are attacking, we are partially relieved. The suspense morphs into pure tension during the first attack, which is thwarted. (See my interview with Greengrass in chapter 24.)

The first close call in *Captain Phillips* is a great example of the near-miss effect from chapter 1. It teases the audience and makes us anticipate the next attack that much stronger.

Later, in the climax sequence of *Captain Phillips*, we are shown the Navy's secret plans to shoot the pirates and rescue the captain. Neither the captain nor the pirates know about the plan, and are told of an entirely different plan as a ruse. But, because we are given an omnipresent view, we also know things that the Navy doesn't know, and that if the pirates discover this plan early, they will kill the captain outright. Because we know more than either side, we feel suspense.

There are times, though, that information should be hidden from the audience. Hidden secrets are revealed to the audience in a surprise twist, like a magician's sleight of hand. As screenwriter William C. Martell says, "a twist is something that has been there all along and nobody noticed until the right moment."

If everything is hidden from the audience, in some attempt to be elusive and clever, suspense probably isn't likely to last long. You may end up with a movie like *2001: A Space Odyssey*—an epic film but certainly not suspenseful. An exception may be the scene where HAL begins to murder the crew. It's filled with suspense because the crew is keeping a secret from HAL—that they're trying to dismantle him.

OTHER CHARACTERS' SECRETS

Take a look at your script again. Are there secrets on the other side? Do the antagonist or supporting characters know plot information that the protagonist doesn't know? Do they hide this information from the protagonist? What will happen if the protagonist finds out this secret plot information?

Letting the audience in on the antagonist's secrets is a powerful way to generate suspense. The movie *Marnie* is a great example of suspense generated around both sides keeping secrets from each other. You have a female protagonist, Marnie, who is a pathological liar and thief, and an antagonist who knows this yet sets her up for blackmail so he can control her. This all comes to a head during their lunch conversation at a diner in which they both confront their secrets. During this sequence filled with tension and drama, some of the secrets are let out, but not all. Since the audience knows about the secrets on each side, the suspense is generated through the drama of their mutual suspicions.

In the Hitchcock TV episode "Banquo's Chair" (1959), both sides have secrets and the protagonist has set up a confrontation scene to get the antagonist to confess murder. Detectives have invited a suspect to dinner and arranged an actor to pretend to be the ghost of the deceased victim, to see if it will cause the suspect to freak out. At dinner, the ghost actor shows up and everyone pretends she isn't there. The suspect tries to stay calm. In this scenario, both sides have secrets. It becomes a game of chicken as neither side wants to reveal what they know. This dinner conversation becomes innately trivial as both sides try to hide their secrets behind small talk. The fake ghost appears, they all pretend not to see it, and the suspense rises. The real gag is on us, though, due to a twist ending that I won't reveal here.

Since a film like director Doug Liman's *Bourne Identity* (2002) is about a protagonist with amnesia, there is an automatic curiosity surrounding the answers to that identity riddle. The antagonists seem to know everything in *Bourne*, and the director chooses calculated moments to reveal it to us before the protagonist finds out. This prelude creates a feeling of anticipation surrounding the revelation of the secret.

MULTIPLE LAYERS IN "YOU'VE GOT MAIL"

Even romantic comedies can thrive on suspense. Case in point is direc-
tor Nora Ephron's 1998 classic *You've Got Mail,* starring Tom Hanks and
Meg Ryan. The film is loosely based on the plot of *A Shop Around the
Corner* (1940) and the 1937 Hungarian play *Parfumerie* by Miklós László.
These stories feature a pair of bitter business rivals who, though luck
of fate, have been writing romantic letters to each other anonymously.
Their romantic relationship has the potential of blowing up if their true
identities are revealed to each other.

You've Got Mail is a great study of suspense writing. It has multiple layers of secrets that are kept between protagonist, audience and the other
characters—the Triad of Secrets. Let's break it down.

▲ **Audience:** The audience is given a secret (Secret 1) that none of
the characters know: we know what both of the anonymous emailers look like: Joe (Tom Hanks) and Kathleen (Meg Ryan).

▲ **Audience:** When Joe and Kathleen pass each other on the street
(close call), they have no idea. And when they serendipitously cross
paths again in the coffee shop (close call), they still don't know. But
we know the secret—and that keeps us intrigued.

▲ **Audience:** Joe visits Kathleen's bookstore and they talk, meeting
in person for the first time (close call). Joe hides his real-life identity and the fact that he's building a bargain bookstore down the
street (Secret 2). Still, only the audience knows that these two are
the anonymous emailers (Secret 1).

▲ **Audience:** Later at a business party, they meet again (close call).
Kathleen finds out that Joe is her competitor (Secret 2) and they
quickly become bitter rivals.

▲ **Audience:** It's when the two online emailers decide to meet in
person that the audience is prepared for all to be revealed. We think
Joe and Kathleen will soon find out the secret (Secret 1).

▲ **Joe & Audience:** At the dinner date, Joe sees Kathleen through the
restaurant window and realizes her secret identity (close call half

resolved). Now he knows our secret, but he keeps it from her. He shows up as Joe-the-rival, making Kathleen think that her online companion didn't show up (close call).

▲ **Joe & Audience:** From this point on, we are waiting in suspense for Kathleen to finally realize Joe's secret identity. The two rivals begin to fall in love, but Joe must find the right time to tell her (close calls).

▲ **Joe, Audience & Kathleen:** At the film's climax, the two emailers decide to meet in the park. This is the moment the audience has been waiting for—for the secret to finally be revealed. It happens in a wide shot (make note of that) as Joe slowly walks into frame from a distance. Now both characters know the secret we've known from the beginning (close call fully resolved), and we finally have closure.

As you watch *You've Got Mail,* you'll notice that entire scenes are built around teasing the audience about whether that secret is going to come out. Those "that was close!" moments are very important for maintaining suspense and nudging our involvement higher.

Deep down we want the secret to get out, but we also know the consequences. The story continues to dance along the tightrope, teasing us, taunting us with the danger of falling off.

COMPLEXITY IN "NORTH BY NORTHWEST"

Let's look at some layers of secrets in two beginning sequences of *North by Northwest* (1959). It has such complexity that is makes for compelling audience involvement.

THE ABDUCTION

While having dinner in a restaurant, Thornhill is abducted at gunpoint by a team of thugs and taken to a house, intoxicated, then released to drive in a stolen car. He is arrested for drunk driving and neither the police nor his mother believe his story.

Audience: We know Thornhill was abducted.

Thornhill: Knows he was abducted.

Police: Don't believe he was abducted.

Mother: Doesn't believe he was abducted.

Abductors: They hide the abduction from police and mother.

Thornhill attempts to prove himself to the police in the face of his lying abductors, creating high suspense.

KAPLAN'S HOTEL ROOM

In order to find out more information about his abductors, Thornhill and his mother sneak into a hotel room pretending to be George Kaplan.

Desk Clerk: Thinks Thornhill is Kaplan.

Audience: We know Thornhill isn't Kaplan.

Thornhill: Knows he's not Kaplan, pretends to be.

Mother: Knows he's not Kaplan.

Bell Boy: Thinks he's Kaplan.

Maid: Thinks he's Kaplan.

Abductors: Think he's Kaplan.

North by Northwest continues as the access to secrets changes with twists and surprises, fully engaging the Triad of Secrets to maximum effect. The audience is given a privileged secret that the CIA is controlling things behind the scenes, and that some of the supporting characters are working for them. In key moments, this is revealed to the protagonist, and later the antagonists. It's only at the end of the film that everyone knows everything and the audience can rest.

BACK TO YOUR SCRIPT

Once you've planted your secrets, figured out which characters know about the secrets, and which secrets the audience knows about, it's time to build those "that was close!" moments. Pitting the three arms of the triad against each other will heighten the suspense and keep the audience addicted to holding on for the outcome.

In the next chapter, we'll help you construct those close-call moments.

SUGGESTED VIEWING

Watch these films and TV episodes mentioned in this chapter to learn more about planting secrets.

▲ *Leave It to Beaver,* "The Boat Builders," Season 2, Episode 16 (1959)
▲ *You've Got Mail* (1998), Dir. Nora Ephron.
▲ *Alfred Hitchcock Presents*, "Banquo's Chair," Season 4, Episode 29 (1959)
▲ *The Bourne Identity* (2002), Dir. Doug Liman.
▲ *North by Northwest* (1959)

FURTHER READING

Auiler, Dan 2001. *Hitchcock's Notebooks: An Authorized and Illustrated Look Inside the Creative Mind of Alfred Hitchcock*, Harper Collins, New York.
Gottlieb, Sidney 2003. *Alfred Hitchcock Interviews*, University Press Mississippi, Jackson.

SUSPENSE MYTH NO. 2

MY VILLAIN MUST BE EVIL INCARNATE

Nope. According to Hitch, audiences can't relate to professional criminals, serial killers and other extremes of uncomplicated, mindless evil. And if they can't relate, they won't feel suspense.

Allow your audience to have empathy with your villain. When your audience starts to care about the bad guy, they will feel the story on a deeper level. Hitchcock revolutionized this narrative boundary between good and evil, making both sides imperfect and vulnerable to making mistakes. Think of it as a football game—you might not like the opposing team, but you appreciate their skills, and would feel sorry for them if they lost.

A villain placed into your story only as a cardboard placeholder to give the hero something to fight against is not a suspenseful villain. Some of Hitchcock's best villains are personable, funny and easygoing—remember Joseph Cotten in *Shadow of a Doubt?*—and we believe in the logic behind their goals. After all, as Hitch once said, the more successful the villain, the more successful the picture. ◢

CHAPTER 3

SUSPENSE MODELS

IF YOU'VE FOLLOWED THE PREVIOUS CHAPTERS, you're now armed with your plot secrets and are ready to implement suspense in your movie. You've determined which people in the Triad of Secrets know about the secrets, and are ready to start pitting them against each other to let that secret out.

It's time to build in some "that was close!" moments to tease the audience with the secrets. It all seems pretty clear up to this point. But the act of setting up these suspense scenarios can get a little tricky.

In this chapter I've outlined some prominent suspense models used by the Master, Alfred Hitchcock. Read through them and see if any of them might be a good match to your story.

If none of the suspense models outlined in this chapter seem similar to your script, it might be a daunting idea to try to incorporate one of them for suspense. Start simple. Because suspense works on basic instincts and universal moments of fear, it's useful to go back to childhood and find elements that would be a part of the child's world. These fears tend to be universal and are prime candidates for suspense setups.

Here's a list of some childhood suspense moments. Notice how many of these are part of Hitchcock films?

- ◢ Eavesdropping
- ◢ Hiding in a secret spot and waiting to be found by someone, and holding back giggles when they get close

- Afraid of parents or teachers catching you doing something wrong
- Lying to parents/teachers when they do catch you
- Being falsely accused of something you didn't do and unable to convince anyone of your innocence
- Being afraid to talk to a stranger
- Getting lost in a store, unable to find parents
- Anticipating a surprise party or gift

Now take a look at your script and see if there are any ways for your characters to do something similar to those moments listed. Can your protagonist eavesdrop on another character and find out information that could change everything? Should they keep that secret to themselves, but be tempted to let it out? Will they get caught eavesdropping?

Now take a look at the suspense models outlined below and see if you can weave any of those secrets into your story somehow. These models are all similar, in that they surround close-call scenarios. Some surround secrets that shouldn't get out, but some are secrets that we *want* to get out but are held back. All are a form of dance between the parts of the Triad of Secrets. Suspense is raised by generating enjoyable frustration in the viewer and calling upon those rescue instincts.

Writing these can be a fun process and intimidating, too, because it can unravel the work you've already done writing your script. If you want suspense, this shake-up might be necessary to involve the audience in your storytelling experience.

Then, at the end of this chapter, we'll show you how you can combine these into multiple layers of secrets by taking a look at *Psycho* (1960).

HERBERT SUSPENSE MODEL

The Herbert Suspense Model is by far the most basic model for plotting out a suspense scenario. It starts with a secret that risks getting out, and a "close call" moment that keeps the audience squirming. The emphasis here is on the buildup to a future event.

1. **Secret Plan:** The filmmaker starts by revealing to the audience a secret plan that the protagonist intends to carry out.

2. **Wait Nervously:** The protagonist then goes through normal activities but must hide his anxiety about the secret plan. The victim of the plan should be around him, pushing his buttons, creating close calls.

3. **Comic Delays:** As the plan is about to be implemented, a series of trivial delays interrupts the protagonist. Even better if the victim is the cause of these delays. NOTE: The victim still has no idea the plan exists.

4. **Almost Caught:** The plan has been carried out, but it goes wrong. There's one last scene that gives the audience an excruciating close-call moment.

The key to this suspense model is the comedy, which creates a fun balance between tension and laughs.

This suspense model is named after the character in Hitchcock's TV episode "Back for Christmas" (1956), in which Herbert plans to murder his wife and bury her in the basement. Once he does it, some friends stop by unexpectedly while he's still cleaning the crime scene.

Because you've made the protagonist nervous in the beginning, and then created some sympathy with comic delays, the audience is automatically on his side. You build the audience up so much that any threat of Herbert's getting caught heightens the suspense.

SAM SUSPENSE MODEL

The Sam Suspense Model is similar to the Herbert model above, but with a slight change in emphasis. Rather than nervously building up to a future event, the event happens first, and the emphasis is on the cover-up.

1. *Withhold Info:* The filmmaker starts by withholding information from the audience to pique their interest. This is very short-lived but prepares them for the big reveal.
2. *Hero Does Wrong:* The protagonist does something which must be hidden from everyone. Since the audience now suddenly knows, we share the secret.
3. *Long Cover-Up:* The protagonist goes through a thoughtful process of covering up all evidence of what he's done. This builds empathy in the audience. The more time we invest in his cover-up, the stronger the suspense will be later.
4. *Almost Caught:* This scenario gives the audience a series of "that was close!" moments. Something trivial becomes the focus of suspense rather than the actual secret.

The key to the Sam Suspense Model is choosing a trivial object of focus that acts as a surrogate for the real secret. Creating suspense around the real secret would be clichéd and expected. Don't do that.

This suspense model is named after the character in Hitchcock's TV episode "One More Mile to Go" (1957), in which Sam has hidden his wife's body in the car trunk and goes for a drive. The focus on the long, detailed cover-up is what solidifies empathy in the audience. And, much like Marion's theft and the policeman's pursuit in *Psycho* (1960), it is a pesky motorcycle cop that obsesses over Sam's broken taillight that generates suspense. The taillight becomes the focus rather than the missing wife.

The same scenario was used again in Hitchcock's TV episode "Lamb to the Slaughter" (1958) in which Mary has killed her husband with a frozen leg of lamb. She then cooks the lamb for dinner and feeds it to investigating detectives. The detectives wonder why they can't find the murder weapon. The leg of lamb becomes the focus of the suspense and Mary's insistence on cooking it is great comedic counterbalance.

In both examples, the protagonist's anxiety rises as the police get close to finding key evidence. But, because of their incompetence, or misplaced trust in the suspect, they miss what's right in front of them.

The audience feels at any point the police may get smart and figure it all out. We hope they don't, but would be equally amused if they did.

INVISIBLE DANGER MODEL

This is a type of suspense setup that builds a "that was close!" moment out of the entire film. It starts with a threat that is invisible and constant close-call moments to remind the audience of the danger at every turn.

Various hidden dangers that could use this suspense technique: a broken elevator that could fall, a live wire that could electrocute someone, a shark threatens beach-goers, or being trapped in a buried car that could cave in, like William Dickerson's *Detour* (2013). (See Dickerson's Q&A at the back of this book.)

1. *Hidden Danger:* The filmmaker starts by revealing to the audience a danger that can't be seen. The danger is preventing the protagonist from escaping the situation.
2. *Delayed Help:* The protagonist waits nervously, hoping to be rescued, or to find a way around this danger before it strikes. Delays caused by incompetent rescuers help build tension.
3. *Delicate Procedure:* A complicated and delicate procedure must be carried out to render the danger neutral. As the plan is implemented, tension is built around the threat of a mistake being made that could trigger the danger to strike.
4. *Twist or Reversal:* The rescue plan has been carried out, but it turns out the danger was never really there. There's one last scene that reveals a new danger, or a surprising return of the real threat.

The key to this suspense model is in "poking the tiger," keeping the threat alive by provoking it often. This suspense technique was coined by screenwriter William C. Martell as a way of elongating the "that was close!" moment into a series of moments that can last through a whole movie.

Martell says, "Suspense is the anticipation of a known action, but the audience might forget about it over time. What you need to do is poke the tiger. Remind the audience that there's that fear of being bitten." And because the danger is off-screen, suspense is generated within the audience's imagination.

Think *Jaws*. "We don't know where that shark is," says Martell. "It could be anyplace and attack anytime. That creates dread in the audience."

This suspense model is used in Hitchcock's TV episode "Poison" (1958), in which a man is trapped in his bed with a poisonous snake under the sheets. If he moves or makes a noise, the snake could bite him. This sets up suspense around a delicate procedure to sedate the snake without provoking it first.

INVISIBLE VICTIM MODEL

Often the scenario is reversed and the protagonist *wants* the secret out rather than hiding it, but they are being blocked. Suspense is generated surrounding the question: "Will they get the secret out?"

1. *Victim Needs Help:* The protagonist is trapped and needs help.
2. *Victim Becomes Invisible:* Something prevents the protagonist from communicating their need for help.
3. *Incompetent Strangers:* One or many strangers are in the position to realize help is needed, but they miss the chance due to being self-absorbed. Often this is exaggerated to comic effect.

In the Invisible Victim Model the protagonist's secret is that he is trapped and needs to escape. He desperately wants the secret to get out so he can be rescued. This suspense setup is the opposite of the typical, where he would want a secret to remain hidden.

So when the second character comes along, this new character has a clear opportunity to discover the secret—that the first character needs to be rescued. The audience sees this as a perfect chance to change the outcome of the story. A close-call moment generates excitement in the audience—if the second person realizes the first needs to be rescued, the story would conclude in a positive way.

But the suspense director instead makes the second character oblivious or incompetent, unable to notice that the rescue is needed. It's right there in front of his nose, the audience is anticipating, yet he still can't see it. This frustrates the audience, because they are worked up to such a level of suspense that they feel like jumping into the movie to fix the problem themselves.

One important element of this suspense model is a lack of musical score. The audience must be able to hear exactly what the protagonist and strangers can hear, as they anticipate any chance of the secret being cued via sound.

An example of this is found in Hitchcock's first sound film, *Blackmail* (1929). When the character Alice is being attacked and raped by a stranger, she screams out for help. Hitchcock cuts to a shot of a policeman casually walking past on the sidewalk below. He happily strolls past without noticing the screams. This incompetence creates a high level of suspense in the audience, because they are rendered just as helpless and invisible as the victim.

For another example of this Invisible Victim Model, watch Hitchcock's TV episode "Four O'Clock," the pilot episode to the series *Suspicion*. A man is tied up in his basement next to a bomb that is set to explode at 4 p.m. He must get the attention of someone to save him, but he has been gagged and can't seem to make enough noise to get his wife's attention upstairs.

Hitchcock then teases the audience with two more chances of rescue as the clock ticks closer to four. First, the gas man shows up and knocks on the basement door. The door is locked so he gives up and walks away. Second, a kid chases a ball near the window and looks in. It takes him a long while to notice the man because he's distracted by a roach walking past the window. Then, he finally sees the man and tells his mother.

At this height of suspense the audience is relieved that the man might be finally saved. Instead, the mother scolds the child for spying into the window and doesn't ever get the message that the man needs to be rescued.

PARANOID CONSPIRACY MODEL

A fun way to get the audience worked up is the Paranoid Conspiracy Model of suspense. In this scenario, the viewer is lured into a wild story that can easily be disproven. Frustration surrounding the protagonist's inability to prove the story is pitted against everyone else's skepticism.

1. *Conspiracy Launched:* Something happens that causes the protagonist to launch into a conspiracy theory.
2. *Skeptic Debunks:* A second person doesn't believe the conspiracy, which causes the protagonist to try harder to find proof.
3. *Cycle of Proof & Debunking:* More evidence unfolds lending credibility to the theory, but the skeptic always finds a way to explain it away. This repeats, each time making the protagonist more nervous.

The audience watching this story is constantly manipulated between believing the story and disbelieving. This kind of suspense is highly reliant on objects that represent concrete evidence.

For great examples of this watch Hitchcock's TV episodes "The Case of Mr. Pelham" and "Mr. Blanchard's Secret." Both episodes feature a protagonist who suspects something nefarious going on. This suspense model also plays a big role in Hitchcock's movie *Rear Window* (1954).

In each of these examples, there is an opposing character that serves as a reality barometer for the audience (see chapter 13). This character helps the audience gauge whether things are real or imagined. The psychologist in "Pelham," the husband in "Blanchard," and Detective Doyle in *Rear Window*—they all serve as skeptics to briefly cause the audience to doubt the protagonist's theory. Then, at an opportune time, Hitchcock reveals proof only to the audience that the conspiracy is true. This fools us into believing again.

MULTIPLE LAYERS IN "PSYCHO"

These suspense models can be combined and merged into more complicated layers. They can stretch across your entire film, or last only one scene. Let's go into more detail by looking at an example from one of Hitchcock's most famous films. Much has been written about *Psycho* (1960), although the focus tends to be on the first hour, up until the body of Marion Crane (Janet Leigh) is sunk into the swamp. Instead, let's look at the latter half of the film, specifically the role of one scene—which I name for ease of description—the Telephone Booth Scene.

This scene plants the seed for suspense for the rest of the film, and creates suspense with elements of the Paranoid Conspiracy Model, the Sam Suspense Model, the Invisible Victim Model, and the Invisible Danger Model.

The Telephone Booth Scene is a simple one of construction, lasting less than two minutes of screen time, and comprising only two shots: establishing shot and master shot. The scene opens wide, establishing the gas station parking lot as Detective Arbogast (Martin Balsam) gets out of his car, shuts the door, and casually enters a phone booth. The booth is standing alone near some trees; a sign reading "Gasoline" is barely seen in the dark left portion of the frame. Dominating the frame is the lighted sign atop the booth which says, in large letters, "Telephone." Arbogast closes the booth door, grabs a notebook from his pocket, and checks for a number.

Hitchcock cuts to the master shot, medium-close onto the booth, as Arbogast puts a coin into the slot, dials the number, and places the receiver to his ear. He then begins his phone conversation with Marion's sister Lila Crane (Vera Miles). Being encased in a glass phone booth, the scene metaphorically functions as a message in a bottle, as it is the last communication Arbogast has with the outside world before he is killed.

The content of this message in a bottle is quite simple, yet precise. Arbogast first reveals that Marion did stay at the Bates Motel, in Cabin One. He then mentions a sick mother who may know more about the whereabouts of Marion. Next, he states his opinion that Sam, Marion's boyfriend, was not involved in Marion's disappearance. Arbogast ends the call by repeating a key point: "See you in about an hour, or less."

Hitchcock's placement of this scene at this precise moment, and his rather objective treatment of the expositional information in the call, gives us insight into his suspense strategy. He chose not to draw attention to the scene, as the information relayed in the call is already known by the viewer. This vital information is meant solely for the knowledge of the other characters, Lila and Sam. Hitchcock then creates a great deal of suspense out of their reaction through the next half-hour, as they refer directly to the call nine times in conversation.

First, Norman Bates (Anthony Perkins) follows the Sam Suspense Model. He's involved in the cover-up of a secret, and faces close calls of this secret getting out.

1. *Withhold Info:* The audience doesn't suspect the murder is going to happen, but once it does it's in our face.

2. ***Hero Does Wrong:*** Norman discovers that his mother has killed Marion.

3. ***Long Cover-Up:*** Norman does a detailed cleaning job and carries the body out to the car to be buried in a swamp.

4. ***Almost Caught:*** He nearly gets caught multiple times.

His first close call occurs when he's covering up the crime scene and a car drives by. He freezes and drops the mop, expecting to get caught. The second close call is when the car is sinking into the swamp and stops before it goes under. Without the car going all the way under, he would get caught. The third close call is when Arbogast arrives to investigate. After leaving to make the phone call, Arbogast returns and gets killed by the mother. This compounds Norman's secret so that when Lila and Sam show up to do their own investigation, the situation is heightened and the audience fully teased.

But the main thrust of the second half of *Psycho* follows the Paranoid Conspiracy Model, as Lila's concern surrounding Arbogast's disappearance grows, yet she has trouble convincing the local sheriff.

1. ***Conspiracy Launched:*** Sam and Lila think something has happened to Detective Arbogast.

2. ***Skeptic Debunks:*** Sheriff isn't concerned.

3. ***Cycle of Proof & Debunking:*** They find new reasons to be worried, but the sheriff still doesn't believe them.

It creates an upswell of forward momentum for the viewer through frantic repetition and the sheriff's aloof circular logic. Worry, wide-eyed speculation and frenzied frustration grow exponentially within Lila and Sam as Hitchcock winds up the tension tighter and tighter toward *Psycho's* climax—all because of Arbogast's phone call.

The audience also follows the Invisible Victim Model as it relates to Arbogast and the call, since we know more than Lila does. We see Arbogast go back to the Bates house and get murdered, a fact that only we know about.

1. *Victim Needs Help:* Arbogast is killed.
2. *Victim Becomes Invisible:* Since he's dead, he can't call for help, except for that phone call he made before the murder.
3. *Incompetent Strangers:* Sheriff is in a position to help, but just isn't interested in looking into it.

Naturally, Arbogast is unable to tell anyone of his murder, so the information in his phone call becomes the surrogate for suspense. The information in the phone call becomes the only hope for the secret to get out—so the authorities will come to the hotel, find the bodies, and arrest Bates and/or his mother. Since the audience is primed with this secret knowledge, it generates suspense as Lila gets closer to finding it.

Hours pass without Arbogast's return, prompting Sam and Lila to take action. As they arrive at the motel, things shift toward a fourth Invisible Danger Model. Both the protagonists and the audience know about the danger. We know the mother has killed, but we don't know where she is. So as Lila enters the house, we are worried that the danger could strike at any moment.

1. *Hidden Danger:* As Lila enters the house, we know she is likely to be killed, but we don't know where.
2. *Delayed Help:* Sam is arguing with Norman outside, trying to distract him so he doesn't come in yet. Sheriff still isn't coming.
3. *Delicate Procedure:* Lila snoops around the house, seeing details of the mother's presence. Each step could provoke the mother to jump out and kill.
4. *Twist or Reversal:* Mother's body is found in the basement. The danger returns in a twist (which I won't reveal here).

Each detail of Lila's exploration of the house becomes suspenseful. As Sam and Norman approach the house, Lila hides in the basement where she confronts the hidden danger and surprise twist.

None of this would have been possible without that simple phone call in the film. Lila wouldn't know where to go, nor about the mother, nor whether to trust Sam. And without her and Sam rushing to the rescue of the missing detective, they would never discover the truth. Clearly, then, this phone call was narratively essential to put things in motion.

Emotionally, the scene is about Arbogast being unsure of how to proceed, being lost, and hoping to "pick up the pieces." It is in the midst of this phone call that he decides to return to the Bates Motel for further investigation. Perhaps in the process of verbalizing the findings to Lila, he begins to have a sense of guilt about not asking more questions of Bates. Of course, if he had stayed and tried to talk to the mother, Bates would not have been able to climb to the bedroom and transform himself into the mother, wielding a knife. The very fact that Arbogast leaves temporarily to make this call seals his own fate. The phone booth, with its wire-mesh window, becomes a metaphorical trap from which he cannot escape.

WHAT'S NEXT?

To sum it up: You've planted a secret within your story-world, and then built in some "that was close!" moments to tease the audience about that secret getting out. After a few of those close calls and heightened suspense, you'll want to resolve it with a sleight-of-hand—a surprise twist that leaves the audience amused that the expected outcome didn't occur.

Now that you've incorporated a suspense scenario into your script, you'll need to figure out how to shoot it. In Part Two we'll explore the visual language of putting suspense onto the screen with a camera.

SUGGESTED VIEWING

▲ *Alfred Hitchcock Presents*, "Back for Christmas," Season 1, Episode 23 (1956)
▲ *Alfred Hitchcock Presents*, "One More Mile to Go," Season 2, Episode 28 (1957)

▲ *Alfred Hitchcock Presents*, "Poison," Season 4, Episode 1 (1958)
▲ *Suspicion*, "Four O'Clock," Season 1, Episode 1 (1957)
▲ *Alfred Hitchcock Presents*, "Mr. Blanchard's Secret," Season 2, Episode 13 (1956)
▲ *Psycho* (1960)—last half.

FURTHER READING

Bays, Jeffrey 2004–14. *Film Techniques of Alfred Hitchcock*, website, *Borgus.com*.
Bays, Jeffrey 2013. *How to Turn Your Boring Movie into a Hitchcock Thriller*, Borgus Productions.
Bays, Jeffrey 2014–17. *Hitch20*, web-series, YouTube.

PART TWO
LEARNING THE
VISUAL LANGUAGE

CHAPTER 4
WRITING A VISUAL SENTENCE

A WOMAN'S HAND is holding a metal key.

Cut to: the woman's worried face.

With those two images we've already forged the beginnings of a cinematic story. A woman is thinking about this key and what she can do with it. Even without knowing the context of these shots, we can begin to piece together a certain logic and emotion from their juxtaposition.

Once you have your suspense secret planted into your film, you've decided when to reveal that secret to the audience, and you've created close-call scenes to tease the audience with the prospect of that secret getting out, the next step is figuring out how to put all that in front of the camera. This will be the key in building empathy and luring the viewer into the secretive world of your characters. In order to do this you'll have to learn how to write a visual sentence. The next three chapters will help you do just that.

When you're making a film, the least important aspect of your craft is what the characters actually say. The best way to get the audience lured into the secrets of the protagonist is to do so through visual means. Hitchcock said films should be photographs of people *thinking*, rather than talking (Wheldon). It is through the reaction shots of people listening and thinking that we pick up on the subtext—the real meat of what's going on. Often the dialogue is a cover for whatever is being hidden.

> *Dialogue should simply be a sound among other sounds, just something that comes out of the mouths of the people whose eyes tell the story in visual terms.*—ALFRED HITCHCOCK (Truffaut)

When crafting your dialogue, make sure it calls attention to a glance, a hesitation, or an embarrassment that draws the audience into a secret.

Just like a kindergartner learns how to write their first sentences on a chalkboard, the filmmaker and screenwriter must learn the language of the camera. Every shot that you create with the camera is a word, and when the shots are put next to each other in sequence you have a sentence.

Consider this setup: A man has killed his wife. He needs to figure out a way to hide the body. As the director/screenwriter, how do we show this man's thought process?

I think the temptation among a lot of us would be to objectively show his steps. We watch him put the body into the trunk of the car and then go bury it somewhere. By the process of watching him, we anticipate what he might do next. Throw in some complications to make it more tense, and, voilà!

Audience yawns.

Instead, to do it the Hitchcockian way, we have to find a way into his mind and show his decision-making process. As the audience we have to get intimately involved in his cover-up. We have to feel like we've helped him with it. This is what screenwriter William C. Martell calls the "skin jump."

That's where the visual sentence comes into play. You've heard it's important in film to "show not tell," but what does that really mean?

Hitchcock often said that cinema is a "universal language" because every culture of the world can understand it. He said that with any of his films you should be able to turn the sound off and still clearly make sense of the story. The viewer's own native language is superseded by purely visual concepts expressed on the screen.

By constructing sequences of shots that work together, you can spell out specific ideas. Just like words on a page combine to form sentences, you can put together camera shots that convey a logical narrative.

THE BASIC SIMPLE SENTENCE

Don't overthink it.

You have to learn to start thinking on a simple level. Being simplistic gives your film a level of stark clarity that unites all of your viewers. They start feeling the same, and before long (if they're in a theater) the whole room is united with raw anticipation.

Let's start with a basic simple sentence.

Here's an example of a simple sentence from Hitchcock's TV episode "One More Mile to Go" (1957).

> **SHOT 1:** A man looks at something off-screen left.
> **SHOT 2:** A burlap sack hangs on the wall.
> **IMPLIED THOUGHT:** "There's a burlap sack."

These two shots are intercut to create the idea that the man sees a burlap sack (fig. 4.1). The man looks; he sees a burlap sack. Very simple. The audience easily follows along with the logic and it can now be expanded upon.

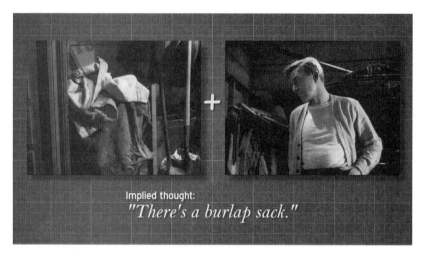

Figure 4.1. Basic Simple Sentence – A simple thought is conveyed by editing two shots of a man looking at a burlap sack. "One More Mile to Go," *Alfred Hitchcock Presents*, ©1957 NBCUniversal.

THE BASIC COMPOUND SENTENCE

Now let's take the same shots from above and add a third shot, so the man alternates between two objects.

SHOT 1: A burlap sack hangs on the wall.
SHOT 2: A man alternates looking between the floor and the wall.
SHOT 3: His wife's body is laying on the floor.
IMPLIED THOUGHT: "Maybe I can put my wife's body into the burlap sack."

The man looks at the body on the floor, then he looks back at the burlap sack, then looks back at the body (fig. 4.2). We see him processing this logic in real time—that he might be able to fit the body into the sack. In my workshops this part is usually where I hear a soft and bewildered "wow!" from the crowd. Yes, it's that simple. Think on a very simple level and build ideas on top of ideas like this throughout your sequence.

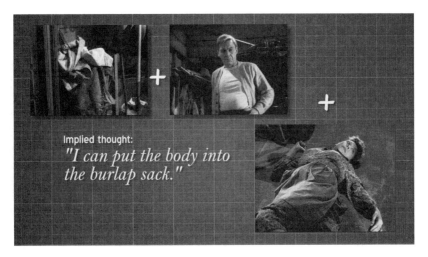

Figure 4.2. Basic Compound Sentence – Adding a second idea to the visual sentence conveys added meaning. The man now has something he can with the burlap sack. "One More Mile to Go," *Alfred Hitchcock Presents*, ©1957 NBCUniversal.

Next the man puts the body into the burlap sack, providing closure on the idea. He tries it out and it works. We feel a sense of shared experience. We now have an internalized investment in the scene.

> *Without speaking, you can show his mind at work, comparing things. There's complete freedom. It's limitless.*—ALFRED HITCHCOCK (Bogdanovich)

THE POV SENTENCE

If you're wondering what all of this has to do with suspense, it's that the more closely the viewer can follow the character's logic (plus the director's logic) and the more present they feel *in the moment,* the more suspense they'll feel as things progress. It allows the audience to connect with the character emotionally.

The next level of visual sentence involves the actual point-of-view of the character. It follows this basic construction:

SHOT 1: He looks.
SHOT 2: He sees (POV shot).
SHOT 3: He wonders.
IMPLIED THOUGHT: (Whatever is in Shot 2.)

With three shots put together sequentially, you convey the story that the character looks, he sees, and then he wonders. This is then repeated as the thought process advances. The first shot is generally a medium–close shot of a character noticing something off-screen. This provides the eye line to cut away to his point-of-view, showing exactly what he sees in the next shot. The third shot is either a return to the first medium–close shot or an even closer shot of his reaction to what he has just seen.

Hitchcock called this "pure cinema." Pure cinema is a focus on the subjective mindset of the character by way of reaction shot. What is he thinking? What is he worried about? Does he notice anything in the room, or something suspicious about the person he's talking to? Reaction shots are a way to let the audience share an experience on screen with the character.

Let's use *Rear Window* (1954) as the classic example (fig. 4.3). He *looks* out the window. He *sees* a man digging in his garden. He *wonders* what the man is up to. *Rear Window* was constructed almost entirely like this.

Figure 4.3. Pure cinema in *Rear Window* (1954). 1) He looks, 2) he sees, 3) he wonders. *Rear Window* ©1954 Paramount Pictures.

Because you're following the eyes of one of the characters, it's like being in the same room with them. Imagine you're standing there talking to the Jeffries character and you notice he's distracted by something off to the side. You would instinctively look, too. Then, you would look back at him to share the experience, to process together what has been seen. The only difference here is that Jeffries doesn't look back at you. In that moment you feel *you are Jeffries.* You've stepped in for him.

And thus, you're more involved in the story.

THE POWER OF KULESHOV

The magical thing about constructing visual sentences like this is that the "words" can easily be replaced to change the entire meaning.

Director and film theorist Lev Kuleshov discovered this in the 1920s and it has since been referred to as the Kuleshov Effect.

Let's go back to the example from *Rear Window.* If we insert a shot of Miss Torso instead of the man in his garden, suddenly we think Jeffries is lusting after the woman (fig. 4.4). The surrounding shots didn't change, but somehow we perceive his thoughts differently. That's the power of Kuleshov.

Figure 4.4. By changing only the contents of the middle shot, Jeffries seems to have changed his attitude, via the Kuleshov Effect. *Rear Window* ©1954 Paramount Pictures.

He *looks* out the window. He *sees* a scantily clad woman doing acrobatics while making breakfast. He *wonders* about the limits of her multitasking skills.

Visual sentences can get even more complex and they can even create people and places that don't exist. Kuleshov discovered that if you use close-ups of various parts of different women's bodies—lips, legs, back, eyes—and edit them sequentially, the multiple women merge into one woman. The mind imposes its own continuity onto the disparate shots. A new woman is created (Kuleshov). This is why stunt doubles have careers.

The same goes for locations. Kuleshov once filmed two people walking through Moscow. They turn to enjoy the scenery. Kuleshov inserted a shot of the White House in Washington D.C. Next, back on the two in Moscow, they walk up the steps of a local church. But, because of the power of editing, the audience feels like they're walking up the White House steps (Kuleshov). Here's how Kuleshov explained it in his 1929 essay "Art of Cinema": "This particular scene demonstrated the incredible potency of montage, which actually appeared so powerful that it was able to alter the essence of the material."

The visual sentence is more powerful than the script! They knew this in the 1920s and it's still true today.

THE ESTABLISHING SHOT SENTENCE

Now I'm going to describe a famous shot from one of Hitchcock's movies, and you tell me what the visual sentence is:

> *A crowded ballroom is seen from above, filled with dancing people. We track down a stairwell over the room, getting closer to eye level. The camera tracks toward a woman, then down to her hand. In her hand is a metal key. Cut to: a reaction shot of the woman's face.*

What's the visual sentence there?

Without knowing anything about the story or the plot, we can piece together a simple idea from this sequence.

The visual sentence would be: "Here's a room full of people that don't know about this key, but the key is very important to the woman."

Don't mistake this classic shot from Hitchcock's *Notorious* (1946) as a showboating establishing shot just for the sake of a director being cool. It's telling a story—a visual story. The director is speaking to us with his *camera*. He's also playing with hidden secrets.

Now I'm going to give you a visual sentence and you decide how to shoot it: "Here's a sunny beach full of happy people, but there's something weird going on in that nearby house." How would you portray this on screen?

Perhaps you would start wide on the beach and then track toward someone walking toward the house. We follow along as she walks into the house. The house is dark and the shades are drawn.

Every shot or sequence of shots in your film should be boiled down to a visual sentence. If the shots aren't saying anything specific, you're probably going to lose the viewer. This is especially true in dialogue scenes where filmmakers choose the standard over-the-shoulder setup.

When it comes to writing and directing, the primary avenue of conveying your story is through the camera. Master that, and you're on your way to finding a stronger bond with your audience.

CREATING VISUAL PARAGRAPHS

Now, imagine this opening of a film written in visual sentences.

People are playing on the sunny beach, but a woman dressed in a pantsuit and carrying a flower walks into a nearby house. She walks in so quietly that the man in the next room doesn't notice she has arrived. She holds the flower and looks for a vase. He's talking on the phone while she eavesdrops. She hears something really important and is shocked. She drops the flower and stomps on it. She sees his wallet lying on the kitchen counter. She grabs the wallet and puts it into her pocket. Satisfied, she walks out in a hurry, forgetting to close the door.

In that example, the visuals speak such volumes that dialogue isn't necessary. Without even knowing what was said, we know that it prompted her to steal the man's wallet. The audience is immediately engaged because we know she has the wallet. We know that all of those people playing on the beach have no idea what just happened. We also know that the man has no idea any of this occurred. The Triad of Secrets is engaged, and we've done it with purely visual sentences.

How would you shoot that scene as the director? A long tracking shot at the beginning following the woman into the house? Close-ups of the woman listening? A point-of-view sequence of her deciding to take the wallet? Notice how each of those shots has a specific language. The establishing shot isn't just there for no reason—it establishes a contrast between the sunny beach and the shady interior of the house. And it demonstrates that all of these people on the beach don't know a secret.

In the next chapter, we'll go even deeper into crafting visual sentences and the words that can be used.

FURTHER READING

Auiler, Dan 2001. *Hitchcock's Notebooks: An Authorized and Illustrated Look Inside the Creative Mind of Alfred Hitchcock*, Harper Collins, New York.

Bogdanovich, Peter 1997. *Who the Devil Made It*, Ballantine Books, New York.

Kuleshov, Lev 1929 (trans. 1974). *Art of Cinema*, Berkeley, University of California Press.

Martell, William 2013. *Hitchcock: Experiments in Terror*, First Strike Productions.

Truffaut, François 1986. *Hitchcock / Truffaut with the collaboration of Helen G. Scott*, Paladin, London.

Wheldon, Huw 1964. "Huw Wheldon Meets Alfred Hitchcock," *Monitor*, May 5, 1964.

SUSPENSE MYTH NO. 3

WORDS ARE THE MOST IMPORTANT THINGS IN A SCENE

Not if your audience is awake. From the Hitchcockian standpoint, dialogue is just insignificant noise coming out of the mouths of the actors. Something else in the scene should be the focus of the camera. In a scene from the 1936 film *Sabotage*, for example, a character is cutting her food with a knife. Through close-ups, Hitchcock makes this gleaming knife the focus of the scene while trivial conversation carries on about the bad food—calling attention to the character's guilt surrounding a murder.

Hitch often treated dialogue like a composer would music, paying special attention to rhythms, movements and crescendos, as opposed to the face value of the words. He coached each actor carefully on where he wanted a pause, a glance or a nervous stumble, in order to call attention to something visual. So position something aside from the topic of conversation as the focus of a dialogue scene. It could be a secret withheld by a character, a glance accentuated in a close-up, or a trivial distraction. ◢

CHAPTER 5
SYNTAX OF EYES, HANDS & FEET

When we tell a cinematic story, we should resort to dialogue only when it's impossible to do otherwise.—ALFRED HITCHCOCK (Truffaut)

AS YOU'RE READING THIS BOOK, what are your hands doing?

Are they holding the book? Holding a highlighter? A pen?

What kind of book is it? Paperback? Electronic tablet?

Now if I started filming you in a scene reading this book, it could get pretty uninteresting.

But suppose I wanted to show that you were nervous. That highlighter, the pen, your stray fingers—all can be cinematic ingredients to express that your character is anxious. You've just been introduced to some new "words" you can use in the syntax of your visual sentences.

If writing a visual sentence requires words, where's the dictionary? While it would be impossible to list every camera shot and what it means, we can boil the cinematic language down to these three basics: *eyes*, *hands*, and *feet*. Pay special attention to hands because they can interact with important objects.

By putting these basic body parts together as they interact with their surroundings, we can begin to tell a cinematic story. Each body part carries with it a unique set of emotional traits.

Notice in the example above that I was using your fingers, highlighter, and pen to express anxiety—an emotion. Emotion is the primary reason to use these words in your visual sentence. Overusing them can lead to diminishing effectiveness. For instance, showing a close-up of a man putting a filter into his coffee machine means nothing—unless you're trying to convey some kind of emotion with that action, or it's a super special plot-driven coffee filter that will save the world later, or there are secret instructions printed on it. Then, yes, it's effective.

Here are some good reasons to use eyes, hands, or feet as emotional indicators:

Eyes (face)
- Feeling and thinking
- Pursuit of curiosity
- Audience empathy

Hands
- Anxiety and shock
- Grabs and hides objects

Feet
- Confidence and safety
- Connection to setting
- Show personality
- Plot-changing decision is made

Take a look through that list and find ways to combine them into a story.

For instance, imagine showing a close-up of Jane's hand holding a flower. Cut to: Jane's face. Suddenly an emotional story begins, as Jane reacts to the flower. Then Jane looks off to the side. Cut to: a shot of a vase sitting on a table. Cut back to Jane's face, thinking.

At this point we can assume that Jane will put the flower into the vase to complete the logical construct. But, as a twist we cut to a shot of her hand dropping the flower onto the floor. Cut to: Jane's foot stomping on it. Finally, we cut back to her face to get a reaction to what she's done.

In this sequence, we've conveyed a tremendous amount of emotional content with eyes, hands, and feet. We've involved the audience in a choice that Jane made, and pulled them into the moment of decision.

A hyper-present clarity is generated by focusing on the simple goals surrounding eyes, hands and objects, and feet.

EYES (FACE)

Looks and glances. In chapter 4 we said a lot about the eyes and how they're used as a cornerstone of visual sentences.

The eyes can also convey certain ideas on their own. Very often during a nonsensical conversation, Hitchcock would cut to an actor's face listening for a long period of time while the other person is talking. This immediately gives us a sense of untrustworthiness or of a secret being withheld. Eyes darting to the side can show awkwardness.

Choosing an odd camera placement can also create an emotional charge. A profile shot of Elsa in Hitchcock's TV episode "Revenge" (1955) gives us a clue that she may be lying, or delusional.

Even a shot of the back of someone's head can be an effective emotional indicator. In the TV episode "The Crystal Trench" (1959), Hitchcock lingers on a long shot of the back of the protagonist's head during a conversation. She's so distraught about her husband's death that this conveys a feeling of distance and detachment from the conversation.

Hiding parts of the face is also effective, as in Hitchcock's TV episode "Banquo's Chair" (1959). The guilty antagonist sits for dinner while a large candelabra obstructs our view of his expressions.

HANDS & OBJECTS

As the previous example with Jane and the flower demonstrates, hands are the primary means of a character interacting with the objects around them. Hands become a primary driver of plot within the story-world.

By focusing on an object in someone's hand, a director can demonstrate an emotion without showing it obviously on the actor's face. In *Sabotage* (1936), for example, Sylvia Sidney's memory of murder connects with the carving knife she uses when sitting down to dinner. Even though the conversation at the table is quite innocuous, the camera cuts from her eyes to the knife and back as her tension rises (Hitchcock).

SUSPENSE OBJECTS

Objects are everything in the Hitchcock storytelling language. Often these objects are evidence of a crime and carry with them emotional guilt, such as the frozen leg of lamb in "Lamb to the Slaughter." The closer the police get to uncovering this murder weapon, the more tense it gets for the protagonist, and us! So when the police take the cooked leg of lamb out of the oven, you can bet it's in a close-up along with a close shot of Mary's guilty face.

Objects can generate paranoia, like the cigarette butts and beer bottles which Ralph sees in Hitchcock's TV episode "Four O'Clock" (1957). He thinks they are proof that his wife is cheating. Or, in "The Case of Mr. Pelham," Pelham hopes that the bank checks and his new tie are proof that he is real, and that his doppelganger won't be able to mimic this hard evidence. They're also a way for us to track evidence through the story and confirm his sanity.

Focusing on triviality and simplicity is a key element of suspense. When the darkest, most serious things are happening, turn the focus of the suspense on a small, insignificant object.

A proxy suspense object is an object in a narrative that is aligned with the hidden secret and represents an ominous threat toward the story's likely outcome (see chapter 15). In my film *Offing David* (2008), David's phone is charged with such dramatic weight that it becomes its own character in the story. It is a proxy for David's body. Each time someone discovers it, it's packed with the suspense of blowing the whole secret. The phone's mere presence in a scene causes suspense. In *Offing David* it is precisely because the audience has the only clear vantage point of the phone's importance that each "that was close!" moment has such power.

EMOTIONAL HANDS

When a hand knocks over a glass of wine, such as in Hitchcock's TV episode "Dip in the Pool," a quick close-up adds emotional weight to the scene. The character who made the mistake is obviously on edge, being careless, or is overly self-conscious for a reason important to the plot.

Hands can also show anxiety and shock. A finger tapping, a hand squeezing a pillow, or a hand playing with a pencil—all are ways of building the feeling of nervousness from a character. Shock can be conveyed by having a character suddenly drop something, flail out while being choked, or going limp at the time of death (see the oven scene in *Torn Curtain*).

In the TV episode "Breakdown" (1955), Hitchcock takes the narrative importance of hands to the extreme. The protagonist is paralyzed in a car accident and can only move one finger. That finger becomes the only way for him to signal to the police that he's still alive. All of the tension and plot surrounds whether his plan will work, as noise in the area makes it impossible to hear his finger tapping.

FEET

You might remember the opening sequence to Hitchcock's *Strangers on a Train* (1951) which follows feet getting out of a cab and walking into a train station. Another set of feet get out of another cab and do the same. Eventually the two pairs of feet bump into each other and the story begins.

Feet can hold a lot of power in the cinematic world. In *Strangers on a Train*, the two sets of feet convey differences in personality of the two characters. One has flamboyant shoes and walks with a certain boyish swagger. The other's shoes are conservative in style and he walks more pensively.

Shots of feet can also be a dramatic introduction to a character that will make an important impact on the story. When the suspicious brother is introduced in "Four O'Clock," Hitchcock focuses on his feet walking through the doorway. It emphasizes that this character's entrance is significant. Similarly, in "Revenge," he shows the feet of the villain (Carl) stepping out of his truck on his way to murder the stranger. Carl has made a decision that will profoundly change the plot moving forward.

Feet also represent safety and confidence in the surrounding environment. When feet are planted firmly on the ground, all is good, but when they aren't . . . danger is afoot. Take this example (fig. 5.1) of feet and hands interacting in *North by Northwest* (1959).

Figure 5.1. Feet and hands tell a story in this single shot. *North by Northwest* ©1959 MGM.

The villain's feet are standing on Cary Grant's hands while he's hanging from a cliff. In the same shot, a gunshot is heard, the villain's legs and shoes fall sideways to indicate he has been shot, thus freeing the hands. The villain's feet are no longer on the ground indicating that he's no longer safe. Similarly, in *Marnie* (1964), when Marnie struggles to decide whether to steal the money a second time, her feet wobble and spin as Mark tries to force her to face it.

In *Lifeboat* (1944), a man's leg must be amputated, and that's a bad sign for his fate (he falls overboard soon after). There's a memorable romantic moment in *Lifeboat* where a couple is laying together and Hitchcock pans down to their bare feet playfully tickling each other.

Eyes, hands, and feet are vital elements of the visual sentence. With them, you can construct an endless number of stories with emotional emphasis. Once again, it is all done without a word spoken.

PUTTING IT ALL TOGETHER

Remember the example from the previous chapter with the woman stealing a wallet? Here it is again, and this time, think about where you can use eyes, hands, and feet to help tell the story.

> *People are playing on the sunny beach, but a woman dressed in a pantsuit and carrying a flower walks into a nearby house. She walks in so quietly that the man in the next room doesn't notice she has arrived. She holds the flower and looks for a vase. He's talking on the phone while she eavesdrops. She hears something really important and is shocked. She drops the flower and stomps on it. She sees his wallet lying on the kitchen counter. She grabs the wallet and puts it into her pocket. Satisfied, she walks out in a hurry, forgetting to close the door.*

Perhaps in that example you can use a close-up on her face when she hears the man talking and becomes curious. You can use a close-up of her hand squeezing her purse-strap when she is shocked about what she's hearing. Notice that the presence of the wallet allows a simplistic story to be built around an object. Use a close-up of her hand when she grabs the wallet, then cut to her happy face, indicating that she's pleased about her decision. A shot of her feet shuffling down the sidewalk could help indicate that she has made an important decision but is still nervous. This would be a great time for her to be interrupted by a kid chasing a stray volleyball right on her path. The story continues.

Looking at narrative in this way helps write the script, too, because it forces you away from dialogue and toward visual ideas. Once you start putting together objects in a room and allowing your protagonist to interact with them, a story is sure to bubble up.

Remember to only use these techniques for emotional emphasis to tell the story. If you start overusing these close-ups they will get worn out and become ineffective. Only use them to lure the audience into a secret, or when an important emotional reaction prompts a decision. In the next chapter, we'll discuss savoring close-ups and how to combine them with wide shots in an "orchestra" of camera proximity.

FURTHER READING

Hitchcock, Alfred 1937. "My Own Methods," *Sight and Sound*, accessed online Sept 2013: *http://www.hitchcockwiki.com*.

Truffaut, François 1986. *Hitchcock / Truffaut with the collaboration of Helen G. Scott*, Paladin, London, p. 61.

CHAPTER 6
CAMERA AS A MUSICAL INSTRUMENT

Cinema is the orchestration of shots. I, myself, use musical terms when I direct. I say, "Don't put a great big close-up there because it's loud brass and you mustn't use a loud note unless it's absolutely vital."—ALFRED HITCHCOCK (Auiler)

YOU MIGHT NOT REALIZE THIS but your camera is like a musical instrument. *Merriam-Webster's Collegiate Dictionary* defines music as "the science or art of ordering tones or sounds in succession, in combination, and in temporal relationships to produce a composition having unity and continuity." Just like an instrument, your movie camera can combine various intensities of visual stimuli in a harmonic and pleasing way to evoke emotion. This combination happens late in the game—in the editing room—but its inception lies with the director in pre-production and principal photography.

Directors may wish to shoot coverage of each scene from all significant vantage points—master shot, mediums, close-ups, and cutaways. This gives the editor a lot to work with. But a careful craftsman has a working knowledge of what each of those shot proximities does, when each one is needed, and how they work together among the greater rhythms of the film. Rather than random chaos in the shot selection in the editing room, suspense filmmakers can benefit from carefully orchestrated intensities of shots. Ideally, these shots can be prioritized in the shooting schedule in advance, and directors can save time on set by minimizing wasted shot setups.

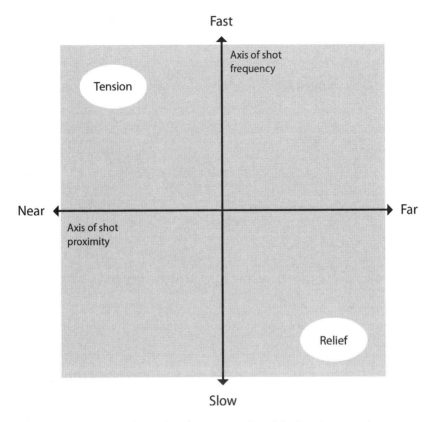

Figure 6.1. Directors make choices along these two axes, determining how close to put the camera to the subject and how long to hold the shot before cutting away.

Firstly, the axis of proximity is the range of possible distances the camera can be from the subject. Close-ups naturally tend to hold more tension than wide shots. Secondly, the axis of frequency is the range of editing speeds. Edits that fly by in fast succession tend to be more intense, and little to no edits naturally tend to be more relaxed. There are important exceptions to this which we'll look at later.

By choosing various patterns between shot proximity and frequency throughout a film, the director has ultimate control over the rhythms of the film's visual "music." He can choose fast edits and close-ups for a tense moment, and then move into wide shots and slower edits for a more contemplative moment. He can choose to stay on a single close-up and not cut away in order to provide a desired emotional emphasis. Or, he can stay on a vapid, wide scenery shot for minutes in order to provide a necessary emotional ebb.

And just like in music, the most important thing here is variety. Staying on one note for too long can cause boredom and aesthetic fatigue in the same way that overusing close-ups can deflate their impact. For close-ups to have power, they must be surrounded by moments of wider shots, and vice versa. As the wise editor Walter Murch once said, change is perception and "without change there is no perception" (Ganti).

Don't think that cramming a bunch of close-ups and quick edits is the path to a tense film. Audiences can only stand a certain amount of tension before it must be relieved and rejuvenated. Failure to be aware of this can result in creating fatigue and boredom in your audience.

In our docu-series *Hitch20* we picked apart an episode of Hitchcock's TV series and counted all the shots he used. Here's the breakdown of "Dip in the Pool" (1958):

- There were a total of 47 camera shots in the 26-minute film.
- 94% of them were standard medium shots.
- Only 3% were close-ups—each specifically emphasizing an important piece of plot information or internal character emotion.
- Another 3% were wide shots, which were either establishing shots or served as a counterbalance for a dolly-in.

This data confirms what Hitchcock always said about camera proximity—that close-ups should not be overused. He believed each time a close-up appears on the screen it will have less of an effect the next time it's used. It's like the high note in the "Star-Spangled Banner." If there were five or six instances of this high note in the song, they would have less and less impact each time. This law of diminishing returns is an important takeaway for modern filmmakers in choosing shot size.

For Hitchcock, close-ups, mediums, and wides were all notes of intensity in a symphony of emotions. They all worked together in order to convey a specifically planned orchestration of visuals.

> *It's about what mood he's in. What's his state of mind? You can only think of the screen and how best to communicate that emotional state of mind compositionally and rhythmically.* —ALFRED HITCHCOCK (Bogdanovich)

IMPORTANCE OF NOT CUTTING

Hitchcock also believed that cutting away from a close-up immediately causes the tension contained within it to dissipate to some degree. That's why throughout his work you'll see protracted close-ups during tense moments, and often whipping the camera to the next shot instead of cutting. See the section below on whip pans.

Holding onto a shot without cutting away allows the dramatic tension provided by the actors to carry the tension of the scene. A prime example of this is in Hitchcock's TV episode "Revenge" (1955), in which Elsa is in shock from just being attacked in her home. She is in bed and stares motionless as her husband Carl tries to ask her what happened. Her response is contained in a long, single close-up, as she stutters out her answer. The result is that we feel how trapped she feels, and we share her sense of shock.

Saar Klein (editor of *The Bourne Identity*) uses a similar protracted close-up in his film *After the Fall* when the protagonist is driving away from committing burglary. The camera stays on his close-up as he begins to process the emotions of what he has just done. Music rises and he begins to have a panic attack, all within the close framing. See our Q&A with Saar Klein at the end of this book which discusses this scene further.

Even if the character gets up from a chair and begins walking, the camera should follow along with them in a single shot, in order to maintain the intensity of their emotional reactions (Truffaut).

Jean Luc Godard once said about Hitchcock that he was "able to assemble the equivalent of several close-ups in one shot, giving them a force they would not have had individually." Godard continued:

> Above all—and this is the important thing—he did it deliberately and at precisely the right moment. When necessary, he will also do the reverse, using a series of rapid close-ups as the equivalent of a master shot. (Martin)

Deciding when to use single tracking shots should be dependent on the emotion the audience needs to feel. Certain sequences can be shot in continuous takes to hold onto tension (Gottlieb). For example, a man walks into a haunted house that has already been established as dangerous in previous scenes. Rather than splitting it up into close-ups and mysterious angles, you can shoot the man's entrance in a single tracking shot. The reasoning: because the man is innocent and the audience should be made to feel that he's innocent. Stylizing the shots to emphasize the creepy house could distract from the feeling you really want to convey (Bogdanovich).

Toward the end of *Marnie* there's a sequence where Marnie grabs a gun and walks down a long spiraling flight of stairs. Hitchcock frames this in one long traveling shot, framed closely on her face. As she walks down the stairs, it naturally turns into an above angle view. Because the framing is so tight and the camera moves to keep her constantly in the frame, it holds onto a great deal of emotional tension. We don't really know what she's going to do with the gun, but the emphasis makes us wonder.

Lingering on a wide establishing shot is also a way of providing relief after a tense sequence, but story should creep into it pretty quickly to build forward curiosity. For a great example of this, watch the beginning of the crop-duster scene in *North by Northwest* (1959), which starts with a 60-second stationary wide shot on the flat plains of Indiana. A bus pulls up to the stop and lets a man off. The shot is so wide he looks like an ant in the frame, allowing just enough intrigue to keep the story moving.

TENSION IN A WIDE SHOT?

On the axis of proximity graph (fig. 6.1), we've shown that wide shots provide relief. But is it possible for a wide shot to contain high tension? Hitchcock's answer to this would be absolutely yes. While the shower scene in *Psycho* (1960), made of fast cuts and close-ups, is the most famous from Hitchcock, many of his greatest suspense scenes consist of one stationary wide shot.

Case in point is the long shot in his TV episode "Back for Christmas" (1956), in which the protagonist faces a "that was close!" moment. Herbert has just killed his wife and buried her in the basement. But in his cleanup efforts he faces a new dilemma—he can't wash the dirt off his hands because the water has been turned off in preparation for their planned vacation. He rushes back down to the basement to turn the water main back on, then as he's rushing back upstairs to the sink, he freezes at the stairway door while the doorbell rings. Two friends have decided to stop by and see them off on their trip. Herbert must hide while they walk in. They'll surely find out the wife is missing.

Figure 6.2. A man hides from unexpected guests in "Back for Christmas," holding a secret that he doesn't want revealed. Composing the scene in a single shot allows this close-call moment to maintain tension within the frame. "Back for Christmas," *Alfred Hitchcock Presents*, © 1956 NBCUniversal.

This encounter happens in a single wide shot (fig. 6.2). The right side of the frame includes the stairway door to the basement where Herbert is hiding. The left side of the frame is a view of the front doorway where the visitors have stepped in. The visitors chat among themselves on screen-left, wondering where Herbert is. Herbert is on screen-right, hiding from them. Tension is built into the composition of the shot—a wide shot on the left, and a close-up of Herbert's reaction on the right. The viewer can look back and forth at ease during this scene and calculate the actions of each side. Hitchcock holds the framing until the guests give up and leave.

Another great example of this is toward the end of *Rope* (1948) as the maid begins cleaning. Within a single wide shot, we watch her as she carries dishes from the wooden chest (hiding the body) in the foreground through the kitchen door in the background. She walks back and forth nonchalantly through each step of this process until she begins to open the chest. Hitchcock uses the tension of this close-call moment and the camera composition to carry it all in a single shot.

A third example of tension in a wide shot is the key close-call scene in *Marnie* when Marnie steals money from the office safe. Framed in a wide shot, the janitor enters the frame and begins mopping, setting up a close-call moment that builds tension through the shot. Both sides, completely unaware of each other, slowly work toward a chance encounter. Hitchcock cuts to close-ups as Marnie puts her shoes in her pockets and sneaks away, but then he goes back to another wide shot as she flees down the stairs, barely avoiding being caught by a second janitor walking into frame.

TENSION IN MONTAGE

Montage, on the other hand, relies on editing in order to build tension. *Psycho*'s shower scene is montage. The word montage holds many varied definitions in the film world. In this context, I'm referring to the common American usage, as a quick succession of shots. It combines quick impressions of the same event into a fast collage of images. The basic idea is that this style mimics the process of the human brain.

When in a room, for instance, the mind focuses only on key objects in a room and ignores everything else. It would be useless to examine every detail of the room all the time, so the brain selects only those things relevant to the current train of thought. As the eyes look around, the brain takes snapshots of each important object and places them within a larger impression of the whole room. Montage then, utilizes small pieces of a scene and combines them in succession in order to convey a whole scene.

Montage is a form of fragmentation. Splitting up a scene into a series of shots edited together provides more control over the timing of the scene. It allows the director to expand the duration of a fast event, to draw out its time on screen to increase its tension. Conversely, it can make an event go much quicker than it would in real time by compressing the passage of time between shots. Because of this time manipulation, it also negates the inherent dramatic pacing provided by the actors and imposes its own synthetic tension.

In the climax scene of *Strangers on a Train* (1951), a merry-go-round is spinning wildly out of control. An old man carefully crawls under the merry-go-round to reach a lever to turn it off. As he does so, we get close-ups of screaming kids and wooden horse heads bobbing up and down. As the ride is shut off, it flies off its supports and crashes. We see a montage of close-ups, which then settles into medium and wide shots. The pacing of the edits slows down as the shots get wider.

> To sum it up, you are transferring the menace from the screen into the mind of the audience.—ALFRED HITCHCOCK (Schickel)

Montage also provokes psychological closure, or gestalt, by leaving out key visuals, forcing the mind to fill in the blanks (Zettl). The *Psycho* shower scene comprises seventy-eight shots but not one of those shots shows the knife actually stabbing Marion Crane. The impression of stabbing is created in the mind of the viewer through the continuity created by placing these shots together, and the added sound effect of the knife. Since the stabbing isn't actually there, the mind must create it to provide closure on this fragmented continuity. The mind, then, is tricked into experiencing the stabbing much more intently than if it were on screen.

> So you gradually build up the psychological situation, piece by piece, using the camera to emphasize first one detail, then another. The point is to draw the audience right inside the situation instead of leaving them to watch it from outside, from a distance. And you can do this only by breaking the action up into details and cutting from one to the other, so that each detail is forced in turn on the attention of the audience and reveals its psychological meaning.—ALFRED HITCHCOCK (Hitchcock)

BASIC "NOTES" OF CAMERA ORCHESTRATION

> Every piece of film that you put in the picture should have a purpose. You cannot put it together indiscriminately. It's like notes of music. They must make their point.—ALFRED HITCHCOCK (Gottlieb)

Now that you're ready to start planning and arranging your shot selection with your "musical" camera, here are the basic "notes" in your arsenal.

MEDIUM SHOT: WHITE SPACE

Framing the character in a medium shot (generally from the waist up) is a neutral position of emotion. This is where your camera should rest when anticipating a forthcoming dramatic event. Medium shots are like the white space on a canvas or piece of paper. They serve as the contrast to the more extreme shots used for dramatic emphasis.

The exact framing of a medium shot is quite variable from film to film, and from era to era. In the earlier decades of cinema, they were much wider than they are today. Small TV screens from the 1960s to the 1990s influenced a shift toward closer cameras overall. Now that home screens are getting bigger, this may change again toward wider neutral shots.

CLOSE-UP SHOT: EMPHASIS

Framing close on an actor's face (from shoulders up) provides more focus on the emotion felt by the character on screen, and thus the emotion is shared more intently by the viewer.

Essentially all important changes in the plot and moments of characters reacting to those changes should be saved for close-ups. If they are overused they will gradually lose their impact, and even more extreme close-ups will be needed.

When to use a close-up:

◢ Intense emotion
◢ Suspicion
◢ Listening
◢ Keeping a secret
◢ Showing the audience a secret

It is quite common for close-ups to be used to show a character listening to another person talking. Reaction shots used in this way allow us to "watch the listening" (Auiler). Because it is sharing a reaction, it allows us to internalize what is being said, rather than the act of saying it.

> The size of the image is very important to the emotion, particularly when you're using that image to have the audience identify with it.—ALFRED HITCHCOCK (Truffaut)

Close-ups on objects are also intense notes in the director's orchestral camera patterns. If the close-up is on a hand or object it suggests a dramatic importance. If it is followed by a reaction shot of the face, it allows an emotional connection with the object to form.

WIDE SHOT

Framing the character in a wide shot (from the ground up or farther away) tends to be more objective. Since the character on screen is belittled to a much smaller figure in proportion to the surroundings, their emotional presence is felt much less by the audience. Wide shots tend to provide a counterbalance to the high emotions contained in close-ups.

Common reasons for a wide shot:

- ◢ Show emotional context
- ◢ Reveal scale and distance
- ◢ Demonstrate lonely character
- ◢ Character is helpless to environment
- ◢ Mood setting or mood shifting
- ◢ Relief after tense moment

There are exceptions to this, of course, especially during transport scenes where a character is moving through geography in reaction to plot events. See my book *Between the Scenes* for more on these emotional transitions.

Figure 6.3. The emotional distance between these bickering lovers is made clear in this wide composition. *Torn Curtain* ©1966 Universal Pictures.

Framing multiple characters in a wide shot can help point out how far apart they are, both emotionally and physically in the space. For a great example of this, see a shot in the hotel room of *Torn Curtain* (1966) revealing how far apart the couple is standing from one another during their argument. The shot (fig. 6.3) clearly demonstrates emotional distance in the relationship.

DOLLY-IN SHOT

By moving the camera gradually closer to the subject, you are basically forming the visual sentence: "Here's something important to notice." (See chapter 4 for more on visual sentences.) If you dolly in to an object, you're giving it dramatic significance. A dolly-in on an actor's face indicates rising emotion.

When to use a dolly-in:

◢ Intensify the current emotion
◢ Emphasize an element in the scene
◢ Reveal a secret

In some avant-garde styles of cinematography, the zoom-in is a similar device, although it tends to have a less dramatic impact. See "Sudden Shock" section below.

DOLLY-OUT SHOT

Pulling the camera back gradually from the subject provides a feeling of relief from intense emotion. You're forming the visual sentence: "Nothing can be done." It tends to provoke the audience into a thinking or contemplative mode.

Function of a dolly-out:

◢ Increase the feeling of helplessness
◢ Dissipate tension
◢ Anticipate beginning of a journey

There's a notable dolly-out at the end of *Frenzy* (1972) which pulls away from an imminent murder scene. The shot tracks backward down the stairs and outside of an apartment building, revealing random people walking on the sidewalk and normal traffic bustling on the street. It provides an objective commentary from the filmmaker that "nobody out here knows what's going on in there."

The dolly-out can also be used at the moment a character has decided to take action in reaction to plot events. As they begin moving into action, the camera tracks out to anticipate their journey through expanses of geographic space.

ADVANCED ORCHESTRAL "NOTES"

These more advanced camera orchestrations should be used sparingly within a film, so they don't get worn out. Generally they should accompany extreme changes in the plot, and are designed to be noticed and memorable.

VERTIGO ZOOM

Hitchcock is often credited as the inventor of this trick shot which combines a dolly-in with a simultaneous zoom out, or vice versa. The resulting effect is an eerie protraction of the depth of field, where the background appears to be scrunching and flattening into the foreground, or vice versa. It's an effective way to emphasize a dizzying shift in the plot, where the character on screen is stunned by his changing situation. In Hitchcock's *Vertigo* (1958), it was actually a point-of-view shot from the perspective of James Stewart's character, who suffers from a fear of heights, looking down a flight of stairs and getting vertigo. In *Marnie* (1964), it's the opening shot of a flashback to Marnie's traumatic childhood.

WHIP PAN

This shot replaces montage editing by moving the camera toward each new shot. Instead of cutting to the next shot, you just move the camera to the next shot in real time. The result is that multiple setups are connected into one continuous shot. The most extreme example of this is found in the film *Rope* (1948), which constantly reframes the camera to encompass Hitchcock's pattern of orchestration. In one scene the camera moves along the line of sight of James Stewart to a close-up of the rope tied around a stack of books, then pulls/pans back to Stewart's reaction.

The whip pan is especially useful in tense standoff situations, where a character weighs quick decisions. It also has a way of emphasizing the reaction shot and calls attention to itself as an important plot moment for the audience to notice. You'll find this technique in many common mockumentary shows on TV such as *The Office*.

SUDDEN SHOCK

Cutting from a wide shot of a person immediately to a close-up of the same person has the effect of providing a jolt. It's a great device to use during a shocking event or a sudden surprise. It's a jump cut that was used midway through Hitchcock's *Psycho* (1960) when Detective Arbogast climbs the stairs and is attacked by Mrs. Bates. Hitchcock often referred to this cut as the visual equivalent to sudden brass in a symphony.

ABOVE & BELOW

It's a very common cinema tactic to use above-angle and below-angle shots as a form of power play between characters—the below shot giving the character a menacing power over the scene, etc. In the context of suspense, they can be useful for creating a sense of disorientation or awkwardness in the audience (Bogdanovich). It's a subtle cue that something isn't quite right in this scene, foreshadowing something more to come. In *Psycho*, for example, the below angle of Norman Bates in his office, revealing the birds hanging over him, is a menacing shot which plants doubts in the audience about his sanity. For a full examination of the many uses of the high shot (aka "above-angle shot") in suspense, see chapter 18.

SLOW PAN OR TRACK TO

As you reveal a special secret to the audience that is being hidden from all or some of the characters, panning or tracking the camera toward this secret is a clear way to draw attention to it. As with using the dolly shots, any kind of camera movement should be reserved for revealing important information or emotions to the viewer. It's essentially like the director saying: "Look over here. I want you to see this."

"DIP IN THE POOL" BREAKDOWN

Here's an annotation of the forty-seven shots used in Hitchcock's TV episode "Dip in the Pool" (1958). You can watch further analysis on our YouTube docu-series *Hitch20*, Episode 10, "Dip in the Pool School."

1. Wide
2. Wide
3. Wide → Dolly-in → Medium
4. **Close-up on pills (he's nervous)**
5. Medium → Dolly-out → Wide
6. Medium
7. Wide
8. Wide
9. Wide
10. **Close-up on wine glass spilling (he's nervous)**
11. Medium
12. **Close-up (learns about the game)**
13. **Medium → Dolly-in → Close-up (they gossip about him)**
14. **Close-up ship bow in storm (storm brews)**
15. Wide → Dolly-in → Medium
16. **Close-up (he leaves secretly)**
17. Wide
18. Wide
19. Medium

20. Medium
21. Medium
22. Medium
23. Wide
24. Medium
25. Medium
26. Medium
27. Medium
28. Wide
29. Medium
30. Close-up (he bids)
31. Medium
32. Close-up (bidding)
33. Medium
34. Close-up (bidding)
35. Wide → Dolly-in → Medium
36. Medium (weather is good, didn't win bet)
37. Medium → Dolly-out → Wide
38. Wide
39. Medium
40. Wide
41. Medium → Dolly-in → Close-up (plans to jump)
42. Wide
43. Wide
44. Close-up (closer to jumping)
45. Wide
46. Wide
47. Wide → Dolly-in → Close-up (he jumps, lady doesn't notice)

Even without having detailed plot information, you can make some pretty clear guesses at the plot, just by looking at the close-ups. I've noted in parentheses what the close-ups are revealing, and that gives you a pretty good summary:

The man is nervous which is shown through the close-ups of the pills, and when he spills the wine glass. He learns about a game. Others gossip about him as he leaves the room. He bids in the game. Then, because the weather is good, he loses the bet. Soon he's planning to jump overboard, and then he jumps.

You'll also notice that most of those moments of close-ups are surrounded by camera movement which serves to make them more dramatic. Also note that the most extreme change from wide to close is saved until the very end of the film as the man jumps, revealing the surprise twist.

"Dip in the Pool" is just one random example from Hitchcock's large body of work. It does show some useful insight into his camera orchestration strategy. Mediums and wides are there to allow those important close-up moments to stand out.

Now you've got a better grasp on how to use the camera to construct visual sentences and elicit an emotional dance with the viewer. Your audience will be drawn in that much closer to your characters' hidden secrets and much more likely to feel suspense during your close-call scenarios. In Part Three we'll go deeper into this audience/director dance.

SUGGESTED VIEWING

- ▲ *Rope* (1948)
- ▲ *Alfred Hitchcock Presents*, "Dip in the Pool," Season 3, Episode 35 (1958)
- ▲ *Strangers on a Train* (1951)—merry-go-round scene.
- ▲ *Psycho* (1960)—shower scene.
- ▲ *Alfred Hitchcock Presents*, "Back for Christmas," Season 1, Episode 23 (1956)—wide shot at stairs.

FURTHER READING

Auiler, Dan 2001. *Hitchcock's Notebooks: An Authorized and Illustrated Look Inside the Creative Mind of Alfred Hitchcock*, Harper Collins, New York.

Bays, Jeffrey 2014. *Between the Scenes.* Michael Wiese Productions.

Bogdanovich, Peter 1997. *Who the Devil Made It*, Ballantine Books, New York, chapter 8 (ebook).

Ganti, K 2004, "In Conversation with Walter Murch," *FilmSound.org,* accessed 4 March 2011: <*http://filmsound.org/murch/interview-with-walter-murch.htm*>

Gottlieb, Sidney 1997. *Hitchcock on Hitchcock: Selected Writings and Interviews*, University of California Press, Los Angeles—p. 28.

Martin, Adrian 1992. "Mise en Scène Is Dead," *Continuum*, 5:2, p. 95.

Schickel, Richard 1973. *The Men Who Made the Movies: Hitchcock*, The American Cinematheque TV series.

Zettl, Herbert 1999. *Sight, Sound, Motion.* Wadsworth, pp. 102–103.

PART THREE
THE DIRECTOR GAME

CHAPTER 7
AWAKENING THE STORYTELLER

I have wormed my way into my own pictures as a spy. A director should see how the other half lives.—ALFRED HITCHCOCK

ONCE YOU RELEASE YOUR FILM and audiences begin to watch it, are they going to be thinking about you while watching? Unless they know you personally, or are watching it as a favor to you, probably not. Most people who view a film have no idea who wrote it, directed it, or even consider who was involved behind the scenes.

And that's a comfortable position for most filmmakers. We want the audience to forget they are watching a constructed artifice and to be fully absorbed into the fantasy world, fully involved with the characters. We're okay with the director being the last thing anyone thinks about, as long as people enjoy the movie.

But I'm here to tell you that in the suspense business, that's all wrong. For suspense to work, you *want* the audience to be thinking about the director during the movie. Here's why.

American Hitchcock scholar Thomas Leitch proposed the idea that a successful Hitchcock film is more like a game than a story. A special kind of interaction is invited in order for the audience to enjoy the experience of the movie. Rather than just being a passive viewer, the audience enters a kind of adversarial relationship with the storyteller.

The director becomes a part of the game, an awakened presence which the audience is keenly aware of.

This is an aspect of suspense that I only recently came to. As someone who has studied Hitchcock's techniques for decades, and even made *Offing David* (2008) to put those techniques to use, I'm now convinced that none of it works without a storyteller's presence.

What I mean by this is that the audience should be made consciously aware that there is a storyteller's hand at work. Film is not just a flat screen where people sit and passively absorb the contents. I was recently watching Jim Gillespie's *I Know What You Did Last Summer* (1997) and noticed that he provoked an awareness of his directorial hand. While I wasn't thinking specifically about Gillespie at the time, there is a strong sense of a facetious prankster-storyteller behind the camera that brings you into the game of the film.

Hitchcock knew this, or he stumbled upon it by accident while promoting his brand, and I believe it's the main reason his suspense has been so successful and enduring. Audiences know they're watching a Hitchcock film. They feel his presence behind the camera, and they giggle and point during his cameos. They subconsciously feel that they are part of a clever storytelling game orchestrated by Hitchcock.

He activated this game through his cameos, his personified camera movements, obvious editing, playful red herrings, and clever opening scenes. These all keep that game alive through each film from beginning to end. He was so good at it that we don't even realize he did it. The next few chapters we'll explore how you can do it, too.

WHEN TO USE A CAMEO

Let's start with the cameo, because that's the most obvious thing Hitchcock did. It was the one thing that audiences were consciously aware of, that indicated that there's a directorial hand at work, poking and prodding the story. Since he did nearly forty cameos throughout his career, it gives us a lot of material to assess.

Through his cameos, Hitchcock becomes an ambassador between the audience and the world he has created. Hitchcock scholar Michael Walker's survey of his works reveals that most of Hitchcock's cameos appear at the beginnings of films during scene transitions. They were timed to appear as characters move between locations or just before an important event occurs. The Hitchcock cameo is an omen, warning us that something significant will happen to our protagonist soon. The cameo marks a narrative threshold which, once crossed by the character, cannot be undone (Walker).

Scenes incorporating Hitchcock's cameos include Guy (Farley Granger) stepping off the train in the introduction of *Strangers on a Train* (1951), Uncle Charlie (Joseph Cotten) on the train to Santa Rosa in *Shadow of a Doubt* (1943), and the shift to New York in *Topaz* (1969)—to name a few (Walker).

Crowd scenes were the best opportunity for Hitchcock to appear. There is an element of *Where's Waldo?* in the crowd scenes of every Hitchcock film, as the apt viewer searches for the hidden director. But just like in Waldo, crowds in the Hitchcock world are much more than just a sea of random people. They are filled with intricately detailed caricatures— each with their own separately intriguing story. If the camera stayed on one of these side stories, an entirely new movie could play out equally as interesting as the one being watched.

Hitchcock's cameo, then, allows us to feel a serendipitous moment in which the chosen story brushes past all the others, rising out of the masses to get our full attention. The main plot surreptitiously mingles with these wild and distracting characters, with Hitchcock signaling that he has chosen one for us to follow.

CRAFTING A DIRECTOR'S BRAND

But, if you make a cameo appearance in your film, the results aren't likely to be as effective unless it's a part of your bigger directorial brand. Hitchcock's cameos are tied to his marketing campaigns, and the public character he created.

Hitchcock started appearing in his own films quite early in his directing career, initially because extras were needed to fill crowd scenes. As time went on, his distinctly shaped profile found clever ways to appear in nearly all of his subsequent works. His cameos are more than just self-portraits or an exercise in vanity. They are the branding scheme of an intense publicity effort, and a device to get newspapers talking. He would intentionally orchestrate obvious cameos so the critics would talk more about him than his actors.

He began crafting his directorial image early in his career, even founding a publicity company to get his name in the papers. As early as 1927, he had already drawn up the famous silhouette (fig. 7.1)—the now recognizable pouting lips, big cheeks, and pulled back hair—which appeared in the opening credits of his early films, as well as in the later TV series (Kapsis). His cameos were a direct extension of this branding symbol that helped to perpetuate his persona in the mind of the public.

To further facilitate this brand, he would plant stories in newspapers about his diet. The trick was to get people talking about his weight, and thus consciously visualizing the plump figure that everyone associated with the director (Kapsis). By 1938 he was the most recognizable director in the industry (Van der Poll 2005).

Figure 7.1. Hitchcock's silhouette drawing was a part of his branding image, starting as early as 1927.

The branding image he painted was of a jovial master innocently sneaking around behind the scenes, slyly creating practical jokes for the viewer to enjoy. Leitch described this character he embodied as an "impresario, naïf, fat Cockney, and funhouse architect." This is the persona you saw in interviews, and on TV, and probably the presence you feel behind the camera while watching his movies.

His on-camera introductions of *Alfred Hitchcock Presents* in the 1950s further helped shape his public perception as a director and craftsman. Each episode of his TV show begins as if we've caught a mad scientist in his lab, creating gags and jokes he may try out in the next episode.

During his movie cameos, he feigns innocence as if he's been caught doing something he shouldn't. His facial expression knowingly pretends to carry on with some everyday task, fully conscious of being watched. But, of course, this is all part of the gag—as a wink and a nod to his loyal audience.

Viewers of his films would pick up on it, too, and came to expect the cameos. Hitchcock's cameos facilitate this viewer connection by evoking sympathy, often as the butt of self-depreciating gags. In *Blackmail* (1929) he's being harassed by a child on the train; in *Torn Curtain* (1966) his leg has been peed on by a baby; in *North by Northwest* (1959) he misses the bus; and in *Strangers on a Train* (1951) he has trouble lifting a large double bass onto a train.

These self-effacing gags elicit a likeable giggle in the viewer. Hitchcock is our buddy. He's on our side. He's up there on the screen to get a front row seat of the action—to watch the movie right along with us. But of course the audience knows full well that behind this innocence is a prankster preparing the next tease.

These cameo roles were slightly on a different plane of reality than the other characters, almost like an apparition—they never affected the story. His coy presence is a reminder that he is in control of the film.

And that was the game that he set up.

GAME BETWEEN DIRECTOR & VIEWER

This game goes much further than the cameo appearances. Think of the Triad of Secrets in chapter 2. Secret information being hidden from parts of the triad provoke the audience into involvement. And with the knowledge that the director may hide certain things from the audience, too, it engages our detective hat. We become involved in a game of hide-and-seek with the director.

The ultimate goal of this game is to amuse. Just like when a creepy hand grabs at us in a carnival funhouse, we giggle and laugh because we're in on the joke. We know the experience is going to be full of shocks, face-tious dangers, optical illusions, and that we are the butt of all the pranks orchestrated by all the ghosts, ghouls, and zombies in the funhouse.

That's the relationship that Hitchcock set up with his audiences, and it's why his suspense was so effective. This relationship not only trivialized the horrors to make them more palatable, but it makes *us* the subject rather than the story.

Here's how Leitch explains it:

> [The audience's] suffering does not feel like real suffering but like a teasing game, a necessary prelude to the pleasures they expect eventually and therefore a pleasure itself. In other words, the pleasure audiences take in thrillers . . . is essentially projective and anticipatory, a pleasure defined and guaranteed by the promise of what is to come. Audiences who feel sufficiently reassured by a thriller's generic conventions can enjoy what would otherwise seem like perversely violent, sensational, or shocking stories.

When you're designing your close-call scenarios (covered in Part 1), you'll want both the protagonist and antagonist to have well-defined boundaries. Just like in a football game, each side has certain plays at their disposal and the fans anticipate the strategy. When Herbert is trying to lure his wife into the basement in the TV episode "Back for Christmas" (1956), she must clean house first. In order to speed her up, Herbert must help her cleaning. If he doesn't help, she might get frustrated with him and refuse to go to the basement.

The game is set, and the Hitchcock hand is in full force, shaping, manipulating, and ultimately giving you a pleasurable fun-house ride. You'll be tricked, shocked, on the edge of your seat, and you'll come back begging for more. House cleaning has never been so much fun!

RED HERRINGS

A Hitchcockian film actually encourages misidentification and misinterpretation. It intentionally tricks us into siding with the wrong person, or into siding with a criminal to question our own morals (Leitch). Setting up red herrings to mislead the audience is a key aspect of this audience game.

Great storytellers and orators have known down through the eons that it's not the story, but how you tell it—the showmanship behind it—that makes it enjoyable.

Audiences need to feel that the movie isn't just meandering randomly, that the events aren't just happening "because." They need the satisfaction that the story has an intelligent plan, that there's something profound to be learned from the events on screen, and that the director has found a way to outwit our skepticism and make us feel it unexpectedly. They want to be playfully manipulated and tricked.

A red herring teases the viewer by misdirecting them. It's like a dead end in a maze, or a trap door that leads to a secret tunnel in a video game. It adds to the fun of the experience and makes us feel privileged—that we're seeing something that no one else usually does.

Red herrings are a way to play with the audience's allegiance. Here's an example, from Hitchcock's *The Wrong Man* (1956):

> A man walks up to a female bank teller. Hitchcock cuts to a point-of-view shot from the teller as the man reaches into his coat pocket. The teller gets frightened as the music score swells up. At this moment the music and the framing suggest that he's pulling out a gun. Then the actual object is revealed from his pocket—it's his insurance policy. False alarm. But unfortunately this move causes the teller to falsely recognize him as the man who robbed the bank earlier. She is sensitive to suggestion, and falsely accuses our hero as the robber.

This little red herring plays with our allegiance toward the man, and also gives us a little empathy for his accusers, since we were tricked right along with the teller. It's a brief moment in a scene that goes a long way.

This kind of blatant deception from the director—even going through the trouble to add the ominous music score—gives us pleasure. It's just like the magician fooling us with his card tricks. It makes us keenly aware that the director is actively in there shaping the story.

Red herrings can also be used as a ruse to build suspense around them, like a magician's sleight of hand. There's a fun "that was close!" scene in *The Trouble With Harry* (1955) where several of the characters are in Jennifer's house waiting for the town doctor to come examine the dead body. Unexpectedly, the local deputy shows up first and they all scramble around to hide the body off-camera. As the deputy enters, everyone is playing cards and Sam is casually leaning against the closet door. This door has been notorious for not staying shut. Hitchcock has fooled us into thinking they've hidden the body in the closet. Like a magician making you think the coin is in the left hand, the whole scene plays out with close calls surrounding the door. Sam makes extra effort to keep leaning on it while he's being questioned, making sure it doesn't open. At the end of the scene the closet door opens and it is empty—like the magician's empty hand. Then, like a magician revealing the other hand, Arnie opens the bathroom to reveal the body has been in the bathtub the whole time.

This scenario is a great example of teasing, building a red herring into a scene, getting our worries up and then deflating them with an unexpected yet comical outcome. The result is that our expectations, hopes, and allegiances have been fully manipulated. We want them to get away with hiding the body even more now!

Entire characters can be red herrings. The sister-in-law in *Marnie* is a good example of a character designed solely to lead the audience astray. She gets suspicious about Mark's activity and begins snooping around his desk and listening to his phone calls. This eavesdropping activity is known only by the audience, and leads us to believe she will do something significant to turn the stakes and flip the plot in a new direction. She doesn't. It turns out to be a joke to her, and a great way to lure the audience into the depths of the story.

By activating the presence of the storyteller through a cameo, and perpetuating this presence through red herrings, the audience is more actively alert, waiting to be tricked. This makes them that much more susceptible to be lured into those secrets and close calls that you constructed in previous chapters. There are other ways to keep this directorial presence alive—through the overt personality of the camera and the editing. We'll explore these in the next chapter.

SUGGESTED VIEWING

▲ *I Know What You Did Last Summer* (1997), Dir. Jim Gillespie—watch for his storyteller's presence behind the camera.
▲ *Marnie* (1963)
▲ *The Trouble With Harry* (1955)
▲ *The Wrong Man* (1956)

FURTHER READING

Kapsis, Robert 1992. *Hitchcock: The Making of a Reputation*, University of Chicago Press, Chicago.

Leitch, Thomas 1991. *Find the Director and Other Hitchcock Games*, University of Georgia Press, Athens.

Van der Poll 2005. *Kaapse Bibl*, Sept/Okt 2005, p. 37.

Walker, Michael 2006. *Hitchcock Motifs*, Amsterdam University Press.

CHAPTER 8
PERSONIFIED SHOOTING & EDITING

To CREATE SUSPENSE WITH A CAMERA you want the viewer to stop being a passive sponge for the material and become part of the story-telling game. In the previous chapter you saw how Hitchcock activated his audience's awareness of him through his cameos and red herrings. Everyone knows going in that they're watching a Hitchcock film, and his presence can be felt while watching it.

But, if you're a relatively unknown indie filmmaker and haven't had time to develop a brand and distinctive style throughout a career, inserting your cameo may be useless if nobody knows who you are. Even teasing the audience with red herrings may go unnoticed if the viewer still doesn't recognize your storyteller presence. I blame this as a big reason my film *Offing David* doesn't play well in its opening scenes. Only after the method has been established throughout the first thirty minutes does it begin to be effective.

How else, then, can you impose the director's persona onto the film and awaken that storyteller's presence early?

CAMERA AS STORYTELLER

It's often suggested that filmmakers should never call attention to themselves within their work. It is a common idea that the story should stand on its own without the director getting in the way. Showboating—creating shots simply for the sake of showing off—is discouraged by practitioners and moviegoers alike. The idea is that a self-aggrandizing shot will take the audience out of the story, so therefore it shouldn't be done. After all, if the viewer is spending time consciously thinking about how the movie was made, how can they follow the story?

In the case of suspense, however, Hitchcock clearly demonstrated that carefully crafted, *obvious* camera moves are effective at luring audiences in. Most of his works are filled with self-advertising shots which clearly call attention to the fact that he's the director (Leitch). The reason it works is because, once again, it awakens that audience awareness of the storyteller's hand. It brings alive that audience-director bond that allows the audience to feel like part of a cinematic game.

That's why, even decades after his death, we still clearly feel his presence while watching his films. His personality, felt through his camera moves, was an integral part of why his films resonate.

Take for example a long continuous shot from the opening of Hitchcock's *Rear Window*. The camera pans across a sunny courtyard, passing many apartment windows and people doing various tasks. Then we move backward through a window and look down upon a man sitting in a wheelchair. The camera pans down to reveal a cast on his leg, then pans over to a shelf where the man's items are strewn out—a lens, camera flash bulbs, and a professional camera. All still within the same long shot, Hitchcock then pans upward across the wall to show various framed war photographs. Finally, the camera moves to another shelf where a proof image of a woman's photograph is sitting, then pans down to reveal the same photo on the cover of a magazine.

Now, this shot clearly tells a story: *the man is a war photographer for a magazine. He broke his leg and can't go outside to enjoy the sunny day.*

But who is moving the camera?

Later a similar sequence plays out. The camera stops to watch a cat walking through the courtyard, pans with the cat, then up across the courtyard and down to the photographer's sweating forehead. Cut to: a thermometer showing it's a hot day. It's another great example of a visual sentence (*it's a hot day*), but, again, who is moving the camera?

What's notable about these examples and true for most of Hitchcock's films is that these camera moves tend to have a hesitating pace, as if mimicking the thought and perspective of a person standing in the room. The personified camera thinks, hesitates, looks around, follows moving objects, and stops when it sees something curious.

But it's not the perspective of a character in the scene. It's as if Hitchcock has handed the camera to us to look around for ourselves. A precursor to virtual reality goggles, perhaps?

This kind of anthropomorphic camera movement calls attention to itself big time, but because it's actively revealing story, it becomes part of the narrative. The viewer easily accepts this kind of exploratory viewpoint and doesn't necessarily search for a character to attribute the viewpoint to. Rather, the viewer immediately feels it as the storyteller's hand guiding them through the discourse.

So yes, it is certainly like Hitchcock handing us the camera, but even more than that it's like he's standing next to us saying, "Here, look at this. No, look over there." He's clearly in control, and inviting us to play along. He's designed this little world for us to play in and, like an exuberant kid, is proudly showing us what he's done.

With this personified camera, by the time the suspense setups start playing out, the movie is no longer just characters on a screen. It has become an immersive, director-led, storytelling experience that you can't help but feel a part of.

CHARACTERS ACKNOWLEDGING CAMERA

Characters addressing the audience is common (think *Ferris Bueller's Day Off, The Office,* or any Woody Allen movie) but when it's clear that they, too, are in on the director's game against the audience, that's an even greater level of tease.

The wink toward the camera from Blanch at the end of *Family Plot* (1976) is so surprising that it not only makes viewers self-aware they are watching a movie (placing them in a reflexive stance), but also provokes us into actively wondering how much of what we just saw was a trick. Did Blanch know more than she or Hitchcock let on? How did she know where the diamond was hidden? Is she really psychic?

When we are forced to question everything we believe about the plot and the very storytelling act itself, it puts the audience into a wholly active position. The audience is no longer passive toward the material, and guess what—that means they're not likely to walk away from it.

PERSONIFIED EDITING

When the editing becomes an obvious arm of the storytelling presence, it, too, awakens the bond between director and viewer. This is specifically true when the passage of time and the sequence of events are manipulated to enhance the story. Quentin Tarantino's *Pulp Fiction* comes to mind as a film that shuffles its timeline in a way that provokes the audience to be reflexive on the form.

In Hitchcock's rare TV episode "Incident on a Corner" (1960), the only episode he directed for the *Ford Startime* series, he begins by repeating the opening scene three times from three different points of view.

In the first pass, the titles read: "Here is the *incident*." We watch as a woman breezes through a crossing guard's stop sign and the subsequent argument between the two.

Then, Hitchcock repeats the scene from a different vantage point, beginning with the title: "Here is the *incident* again." Immediately we are pulled out of the role of passive viewer and provoked to become a quasi-detective, examining evidence. It's as if the director is giving you all of his footage and letting you pore over the details. This time, we watch the same scenario, as the woman speeds through the traffic stop and argues with the crossing guard.

On the third pass, we get the title: "Another view of the *incident.*" By this time, the viewer is accustomed to this new format, and anticipates what new details will be revealed in this third camera angle. We aren't disappointed, as this time a second car is foregrounded, and we watch a couple nervously get out and run into a house. Simultaneously, we can hear the familiar argument with the crossing guard playing out in the background.

Similarly, Dan Trachtenberg shakes up the audience with his bold editing of the opening title sequence in *10 Cloverfield Lane* (2016). He intercuts opening titles within a car crash as shock cutaways between each moment of the crash. The sound abruptly goes quiet with each title and then bursts back into the car. The presence of the titles shakes up the audience to such an extent that they are keenly aware of the storyteller.

This kind of narrative construction calls attention to itself by essentially inviting us into the editing room. We become aware that we are watching a film and forced into a reflexive stance toward the material and toward the conventions of sequential time. Through the film's overt editing and on-screen text guides, the viewer is immediately placed into an engaged mode and given secret information that drives our anticipation as the story plays out.

SUGGESTED VIEWING

▲ *Rear Window* (1954)—first few minutes..

▲ *Ford Startime*, "Incident at a Corner," Season 1, Episode 27 (1960)

▲ *10 Cloverfield Lane* (2016), Dir. Dan Trachtenberg—opening titles.

FURTHER READING

Bays, Jeffrey 2013. *How to Turn Your Boring Movie into a Hitchcock Thriller.* Borgus Productions.

Leitch, Thomas 1991. *Find the Director and Other Hitchcock Games*, University of Georgia Press, Athens.

CHAPTER 9

LURE THEM WITH A HITCHCOCKIAN OPENING

It must always be remembered that the primary aim of pictures is to provide entertainment. To entertain people, one must first capture their interest.—
ALFRED HITCHCOCK

AS YOU LEARNED in the previous chapters, your audience should be involved in a game of watching rather than just passively viewing. Adding personality to the camera is a big way of awakening the bond between director and audience. There's no better time to start doing this than in your opening sequence. While it may be effective later in your movie as well, the sooner you teach the audience about the game of watching, the more effective your suspense will be.

THROUGH PUBLIC & PRIVATE SPACE

Movement of the camera through geographic space is one way to signal to the viewer that a new story is being uncovered. Your camera can begin by scanning a public space, luring the viewer from an objective vantage point and calling upon their voyeuristic nature.

Remember the woman-stealing-wallet example from chapters 4 and 5? The opening shot of that scene could be treated as if it's following a random woman walking through a crowded beach. The camera arbitrarily decides to follow her instead of anyone else in the crowd. As the camera follows her inside the house, we are given a secret view into a private world.

Hitchcock commonly used this voyeuristic camera move in the openings of his films, panning toward a private area and intruding. In the case of films like *Rebecca* (1940)—repeated in openings of *Psycho* (1960), *Dial M For Murder* (1954), *Secret Agent* (1936), and others—Hitchcock's camera begins wide on the landscape and moves or pans through the environment in search of a story. *Rebecca* begins with the moon shining through dark rolling clouds, as the camera tracks between the bars of an iron gate. Crossing into private territory, it moves down a driveway surrounded by trees, and soon the camera arrives at an old deteriorated mansion, tracking further around the mansion until it moves in on a window.

In *Psycho* we pass through a crack in the window curtains and enter the hotel room where a couple is getting dressed. Here Hitchcock opens across the Phoenix cityscape, getting closer to the buildings in sequential shots, as if picking out a random window to peer into.

> I'll bet you that nine out of ten people, if they see a woman across the courtyard undressing for bed, or even a man puttering around in his room, will stay and look.—ALFRED HITCHCOCK

It is this free-ranging camera that makes its way more subtly into the opening of films such as *Rope* (1948), *Dial M for Murder*, and *Shadow of a Doubt* (1943), all of which pan from sunny city street and cross through a window to reveal the private space inside.

Opening with a tracking or panning shot like this immediately makes the audience feel special. We feel privileged to have access to secret information and that the director has singled us out. We immediately feel that there is a storyteller actively taking us on a secret tour that no one else sees.

LANDSCAPE & CROWD CARICATURES

If you do choose to start your film in a public space, it will either be empty or filled with crowds of random people. These people should be just as compelling as the main characters of your film. By activating a *Where's Waldo?* type of curiosity, your audience feels that each of these people could have separate movies about them as well. Once the camera finally does get to the protagonist, we feel even more privileged to have access to this specific person. Something about them must be profound enough to choose them out of all these other fascinating people. If only your camera had chosen to follow another one of them, another equally interesting movie could have unfolded.

In the Hitchcockian style, each one of those extras should be comical, ironic, and contain their own interesting stories. The comic Hitchcock landscape is populated by uniquely stylized crowds, portraying the everyday citizen in a rich array of caricatures. An elderly woman glares disapprovingly and a young man whistles suggestively at Tippi Hedren as she crosses the street in the opening of *The Birds* (1963), subtle indications that—we later learn—she has a history of public indecency.

This fine level of detail goes back to Hitchcock's first British film, *The Lodger* (1926), showing a frantic woman recalling a story to the policemen and curious onlookers tipping their heads forward to hear the news. *The 39 Steps* (1935) opens in an auditorium of people gathered to stump Mr. Memory. Hitchcock gives each person a close-up as they take turns asking ridiculous questions, allowing a rich tapestry of personalities to surface.

Hitchcock's extras aren't just generic members of a crowd, they are individuals with their own agendas. We see traders cutting raw fish on the docks in *The Manxman* (1929), bored factory workers on an assembly line in *Saboteur* (1942), and physicists tapping grumpily with their forks at the frozen wine on a cruise ship in *Torn Curtain* (1966).

Grandmothers in feathered hats make frequent crowd appearances, like the woman at the train platform in *Rich and Strange* (1932) losing balance on her feet whilst the tight crowd steps back and forth in unison. On the train a man accidentally grabs the feather on her hat and pulls it off while the train sways; she glares and swipes it back from him. Similarly, the crowds at the beginning of *North by Northwest* seem to walk in unison down the stairs to the subway; a woman tries to get into a taxi before another woman swats her away.

The bus in *The Man Who Knew Too Much* (1955) is packed with tourists: a blonde in sunglasses, a Frenchman, and various veiled Muslims. As we peer down onto the street in *Rope*, we see a woman pushing a baby carriage, another woman sweeping stairs, a man carrying a briefcase, and a policeman escorting two children across the street. *Rear Window* (1954), of course, is filled with a tapestry of comical extras which weave their way into James Stewart's conspiracy.

Lifeboat (1944) opens with objects taking the place of people as Hitchcock pans across various items floating in the water from a sunken ship: a *New Yorker* magazine, playing cards, a checkerboard, and eventually a floating dead body. Dead bodies make frequent appearances in the openings of Hitchcock films, including *Lifeboat*, *Frenzy*, *Young and Innocent*, *The Lodger*, and *The Trouble With Harry*.

Presenting such an interesting crowd not only immediately sparks curiosity in the viewer, it also cues the command and control of the storyteller picking out one person to follow. It's all part of teaching the audience about the game of watching.

FACETIOUS & WHIMSICAL TONE

A comical crowd also starts the film in a fun way, rather than opening with a dreary, dark, spooky environment that would be predictable for a suspense story. Hitchcock believed that all suspense films should begin as comedies (Gottlieb).

In the early part of his career Hitchcock wrote about the need for shifts in tone throughout a film, and that a comic opening is essential to suspense. He said, "in a light-hearted setting, the advent of drama is made all the more effective by its unexpectedness . . . The more happy-go-lucky the setting, the greater kick you get from the sudden introduction of drama." He saw around him that British films had one single tone throughout, yet noted many theater plays had comic first acts which he referred to as "perfect coating with which to sugar the plot-planting pill." In *Film Weekly* he explained:

> *After all, that is how things happen in real life. Although a tragic event may be destined to happen sometime during the afternoon, we do not go about all the morning with somber faces. We just don't know that the catastrophe is coming—consequently, when it does arrive, we are as likely as not to be laughing and drinking in complete light-heartedness.*—ALFRED HITCHCOCK (Gottlieb)

The consequences of not having this contrast between comedy and drama in a film, he said, resulted in a lack of freshness and "unrelieved tension." The drama had no room from which to rise to a dramatic climax. He believed these shifts in mood serve to keep the audience interested and, more importantly, to convey the impression that the characters are first "really alive," leading the viewer then to be drawn into their dramatics (Gottlieb).

A survey of his body of work reveals a growing trend, emerging in his first sound pictures, and especially prevalent in his American period, that a majority of his suspense films opened in the bright daylight accompanied by playful music. With the exceptions of *Young and Innocent* (1937), *Jamaica Inn* (1939), *Rebecca* (1940), *The Wrong Man* (1956), and *Family Plot* (1976)—all of which begin at night—his films tended to open in the afternoon. Even then, in *Rebecca* for instance, the night is immediately juxtaposed by bright sunshine in the next scene, at the beginning of the flashback in which a suicidal man is about to jump from a cliff.

Young and Innocent dissolves from an opening scene in a storm with violent lightning surrounding a couple arguing, to a bright sunny beach in which the woman's body washes up on shore.

Probably the most obvious example of a bright opening is in *The Trouble With Harry* (1955), showing beautiful autumn scenery of orange leaves, rolling Vermont hills, and a church. Then an innocent child skips along and stumbles onto a dead body lying on green grass.

COMICAL MUSIC

Much of Hitchcock's musical introductions tread almost absurdly toward the juvenile, with bouncy flutes and whopping bass tubas, as if he wanted to appeal to our childlike nature. This counterpoint of triviality and danger is fully articulated when gunfire disrupts the auditorium in the opening of *The 39 Steps* (1935), and the stage band plays happy music to calm the crowd.

Even with more dramatic films such as *Rear Window* and *Dial M for Murder*, he opened with a facetious music score, this same childlike peek-a-boo tone recalling his tendency toward audience trickery. Hitchcock openly teases, tickles, and plays with the audience from the very outset of his films, much like one would to a baby (Gottlieb).

If you decide to use some Hitchcockian elements in your opening sequence, you're sure to start curating that playful, adversarial bond with your audience. By opening with a fun excursion from the everyday world into a private, secret space, you'll have them primed for a wild ride of suspense. With continued anthropomorphic camera moves, obvious edits, and perhaps a fun cameo, your audience will be fully aware of the roller coaster you've built for them. They'll enjoy every twist, turn, loop, and red herring, and giggle at your cleverness as a suspense storyteller.

SUGGESTED VIEWING

▲ *Rear Window* (1954)—opening sequence.

▲ *Frenzy* (1972)—opening sequence.

FURTHER READING

Bays, Jeffrey 2004–14. *Film Techniques of Alfred Hitchcock*, website, *Borgus.com*.

Chatman, Seymour 1978. *Story and Discourse*, Cornell University Press, USA.

Condon, Paul and Sangster, Jim 1999. *The Complete Hitchcock*, Virgin Publishing Ltd., London.

Duncan, Paul 2003. *Hitchcock: Architect of Anxiety*, Taschen, Holenzollernring 53, Italy.

Gottlieb, Sidney 1995. *Hitchcock on Hitchcock: Selected Writings and Interviews*, University of California Press, USA.

Smith, Susan 2000. *Hitchcock: Suspense, Humour and Tone*, British Film Institute, London.

Truffaut, François 1984. *Hitchcock by Truffaut: The Definitive Study*, Grafton Books, London.

PART FOUR
THE SOUND OF SUSPENSE

CHAPTER 10
BUILDING A SOUNDSCAPE

BECAUSE SUSPENSE RELIES on such an intense involvement from the audience, sound is a way to enhance that experience and manipulate the viewer for maximum impact. In cases like the basement scene in Hitchcock's TV episode "Four O'Clock" or the song sung by Jo (Doris Day) at the end of *The Man Who Knew Too Much* (1956), the suspense wouldn't be possible without sound. In fact, the scenes wouldn't work at all. As Paul intently listens to the footsteps on the floor above in hopes someone will come toward the stairway door and rescue him, suspense is generated around the progress of the footstep sounds. As Jo sings her song, hoping to cue her kidnapped son to start yelling for help, suspense is generated around whether the son will notice the song, and whether she will hear his response and expose his captors to the crowd below.

Sound in a film is really a third dimension that brings depth to a flat screen. It provides continuity between shots, smoothes out the abruptness of editing, and allows the viewer to become immersed in a fictional world.

Your soundscape can be completely accurate to reality, or it can be manipulated to emphasize certain objects in a scene and deemphasize others. It can be dropped low in the sound mix in favor of dialogue, or it can be purposefully loud to become dominant and overpowering.

Sound can be removed entirely to provide a spotlight on the music score, or to shock the audience with nothingness.

Any choice about what to do with the sound should be made from within the needs of the story and audience. The goal of the sound designer should never be to precisely recreate what a microphone would hear from the camera's viewpoint. The soundscape is a dynamic, living and breathing part of the storytelling machine. It is manipulated to emulate the subjective viewpoint of a character's mind, or to draw the audience's attention to something.

It's ironic that early films are called "silent" because those films (made until the 1930s) were screened with musical accompaniment, often performed live at the cinema. There was nothing silent about that moviegoing experience. By today's standards silent-film music was probably overpowering and distracting, but served the important purpose of filling in the blanks of a film completely absent of a soundtrack.

It's very difficult to actually watch a completely silent movie for any great length of time. The absence of sound or music forces the mind to work hard to pay attention and, over time, it gets fatigued.

The addition of the strip of soundtrack to film stock in the late 1920s changed everything. Hitchcock was among the first in the world to direct a "talkie" picture, a nickname for films that included audible dialogue. The soundtrack opened up a whole new world of creative possibilities and Hitchcock jumped on board with experimentation in his film *Blackmail* (1929).

Blackmail pioneered the use of silence as a dramatic device. Moments that may have traditionally included music could now be made intentionally silent. Ambient sounds could be added to abstract the reality, to push the protagonist, and to let us hear what Alice's delusional mind hears.

Just like Hitchcock did in his first sound film, today's filmmakers should always consider the power of sound in conveying the story to the audience. Here's what sound can do to enhance suspense:

- ◢ Background ambient sound becomes part of the story.
- ◢ Exaggerate a sound to emphasize something in the narrative.
- ◢ Increase tension through both ambient noises and silence.
- ◢ Manipulate knowledge among the Triad of Secrets (see chapter 2).
- ◢ Withhold a sound from the viewer to pique curiosity.
- ◢ Characters make noises instead of speaking.
- ◢ A character must listen closely for important information.

BACKGROUNDS

As you read this, there might be a train whistle, barking dog, or neighbor's music in the background distracting you from concentrating. It's the same in a film. Sounds in a film's backdrop can distract the audience from the story and keep them from understanding important events. Conversely, these sounds can be carefully crafted to clarify the narrative and enhance the viewer's concentration. They can help keep the audience's attention fine-tuned and focused on the progression of events.

Among even experienced filmmakers and screenwriters, sounds that are part of the setting are often not even thought about at the script stage or even the directing phase. It's not until the editing room—and maybe even the final sound mix—that consideration is made on how to fill in that space. You shouldn't wait that long, because you might have missed a great opportunity to tell the story through sound.

Here's a perfect example of that. Hitchcock's TV episode "The Horseplayer" (1961) is about a church that needs to raise money to fix its leaky roof. Now, imagine that's your story. How do you convey to the audience through sound that the church should raise money to fix the leak?

Think it through. A leaking roof means water is dripping in. When does it drip? When it rains. Here's what Hitchcock did. He opened the episode without any music. It begins at a church service, as the congregation is sitting in the pews. We hear loud rain spattering on the roof, and at times the loud dripping sound as water drops onto people's heads. The rain is so loud that we can barely understand what the priest is saying.

As rain drips onto heads, people look up at the ceiling in disgust. We cut to the ceiling, and watch it drip.

"The Horseplayer" is a perfect example of how background sound can become the dominant storytelling device. The sound of the rain becomes so intrusive to our viewing experience that we immediately understand when the priest says he wants to raise money to fix the roof. The plot setup is immediately clear.

Using intrusive background sounds was a key strategy Hitchcock used to increase tension. Bustling street noise and car horns represent the outside world, and when a door opens that sound spills into the room. If the protagonist is feeling guilty and hiding a secret, he may be affected by hearing that noise. The outside world intrudes into his secret space and raises his guilt. This world also carries with it an attitude toward the protagonist, coming alive and reacting to what he has done.

In *Blackmail*, Alice is feeling guilty that she has murdered a man. As she makes the long walk home, she passes clubs full of laughing people. Car horns seem to honk at her mockingly, increasing her dismay. When she gets home, the songbird in her bedroom chirps wildly. These comical sounds seem to belittle her tragedy, and their insistence toward happiness produce an irony that helps bring out Alice's sadness. The contrast helps us internalize her feelings.

Probably the most famous example of an intrusive soundscape is the police siren at the end of *Rope* (1948). It is prompted by Rupert's gunshots. Sounds of neighbors gossiping rise up, and then sirens begin, signaling that the police are on their way. The characters wait in silence as the outside world catches on and the sounds of public intrusion begin to pour into the private apartment.

SECRET SOUNDS

As you've learned throughout this book, the threat of a secret being discovered is key to building a suspense scenario. On top of that, letting the audience in on this secret allows our involvement to be more empathetic. Manipulating sound is another way to reveal or hide these secrets.

The interaction between public vs. private space is important in developing suspense around secretive characters. By creating private spaces to contain secret information, you prevent other characters in the Triad of Secrets from hearing it.

There's a key element of *Blackmail* which exemplifies this manipulation of secret information. A phone booth inside the shop has clear glass doors that can be closed to shut out sound. Whenever a character steps in to make a phone call, no one else in the shop can hear the conversation. Conversely, no one in the booth can hear what's being said outside of it either. Hitchcock makes clever use of this throughout the film. At one point, Frank is on the phone with police headquarters and leaves the doors open so we can hear. Then, as soon as the conversation gets interesting, he closes the doors and all we hear are mumbles. This immediately piques our interest. When the detective finishes and walks through the building, he is armed with that secret that everyone wants to know, including us.

And of course this is the whole idea behind eavesdropping. Eavesdropping is ripe for a level of storytelling that connects to people universally. When a character hears a private conversation through a door, it immediately perks up our attention as a viewer. We naturally lean in to see what is being overheard and whether someone is going to get caught.

Just like the phone booth in *Blackmail* hides information from the audience, the opening of Hitchcock's TV episode "One More Mile to Go" (1957) keeps the dialogue of a fight from us. The camera peers through a window as we watch a couple arguing, flailing their arms, and throwing objects. We can faintly hear the arguing, but not enough to decipher what they are saying. This absence of sound creates intrigue, and provides a sudden jolt when we suddenly appear inside the house at the moment of murder.

HUMAN SOUNDS

Characters can make a variety of sounds in lieu of talking to convey story information. These can all be used during close-call moments to heighten suspense:

- Coughing (disapproval, hiding something)
- Sneezing (breaking silence)
- Whistling or humming (gloating, withholding information)
- Clapping (assertiveness, appreciation)
- Slamming a door (anger)
- Dropping an object (nervousness, distracted)

Can you think of others?

As mentioned in the opening of this chapter, the sound of footsteps in "Four O'Clock" generates suspense in the close-call sequence in that film. Paul has been tied up and gagged in the basement, so he must try to make enough noise to get the attention of his wife above. He stomps his feet and moans, but his attempts don't seem to be working. Not only does Paul need to make sound in order to be rescued, he must listen to his wife's footsteps to time his optimal attempts. As she walks from one part of the house to another, Paul listens to the clicking of her heels, hoping that she will walk to an area closer to him. She doesn't; she walks farther away. Close call thwarted. Then she walks back, close to the basement door. Almost saved! The audience listens to the footsteps and hopes right along with Paul.

Human sounds can also be exaggerated or replaced with the unexpected. In Hitchcock's TV episode "Arthur" he introduces the sound of a chicken being strangled as Arthur kills it. Later, Arthur kills his ex-wife in the same way, but Hitchcock again repeats the sound of the strangled chicken in place of the wife's screams. This automatically connects the two murders with the same sound, and makes the ex-wife seem like yet another chicken.

ABSTRACTED DIALOGUE

Dialogue doesn't always have to be realistic, either. Hitchcock often portrayed speech from the perspective of a character's mind—either selectively manipulating speech heard through their ears, or projecting their internal thoughts as voice-over.

In the famous scene in *Blackmail*, he manipulates the speech of the gossipy neighbor in the shop when she's talking about the knife used for the murder. Hitchcock deliberately accentuates the word "knife" in a repetitive rhythm, mixed with mumblings that were literally spoken by the actress as unintelligible abstracted syllables. This way, we get a clear sense of how Alice's mind perceives the woman's dialogue, subjectively singling out only the one word as she slices the bread. Often a character is talking off-screen while Hitchcock's camera pans toward an object or a reaction on someone's face. Since the camera stays on close-up of Alice during this scene and the gossiper is off-screen, the focus is on the reaction of Alice with each utterance of "knife."

Another ploy that Hitchcock creates with dialogue is missed information, or a sense of misunderstood language in a time of crisis. In *Blackmail*, the housekeeper frantically calls the police, and while she is relaying the address she thinks the dispatcher has heard the address incorrectly. We hear both sides of the conversation and know it's correct, but she repeats the address frantically.

SUGGESTED VIEWING

- ◢ *Blackmail* (1929)—Hitchcock's first sound film, a sandbox of audio experimentation.
- ◢ *Suspicion*, "Four O'Clock," Season 1, Episode 1 (1957)—Paul must make noise to be rescued.

FURTHER READING

Auiler, Dan 2001. *Hitchcock's Notebooks: An Authorized and Illustrated Look Inside the Creative Mind of Alfred Hitchcock*, Harper Collins, New York.

Weis, E 1982. *The Silent Scream*, Associated University Presses, New Jersey.

CHAPTER 11

THE ROLE OF MUSIC IN SUSPENSE

WHEN YOU TELL A STORY, it's not just an intellectual transfer of factual information. Instead, a narrative evokes an emotional dance—a dramatic buildup and emotional release. You could say that storytelling is an emotional relay of ideas.

Since film is grounded in emotion, a music score is a natural component in enhancing the viewer's reception of the story. It has the power to clarify the meaning of a scene event, but it is inherently vague and contextual. As American film scholar Jeff Smith says, music has a "lack of emotional specificity" not inherently clear until it is combined with visuals. Music arises from the context, mood, and attitude of the film rather than simply emoting on the character's behalf.

The presence of music in film is primarily a signifier of transformation to a new state—new scene, new location, new event, new mood, etc. Often it tends to accompany temporal manipulation such as collage, slow motion, and flashback initiation (Gorbman).

Much like scenery, music is one way of expressing dramatic space. It can use a sort of "cultural coding" to evoke historical geographic setting and atmosphere (Gorbman), and it can "activate genre schemata" (Smith). Smith says music can "signify the emotional valence of a particular setting." He uses the example of *Psycho* (1960) in which the old house near the Bates Motel is turned into a "spooky old house" through Bernard

Hermann's score. Likewise, the planet in Ridley Scott's *Alien* (1979) is turned into something more ominous by the mood-setting effect of Jerry Goldsmith's scratchy and howling score (Smith). In some cases, music "evokes a larger than life dimension which, rather than involving us in the narrative, places us in contemplation of it" (Gorbman).

Likewise, Finnish film scholar and architect Juhani Pallasmaa said it succinctly:

> *Music usually has the role of reinforcing atmosphere and emotions in films, creating forebodings and surprises, strengthening a sense of reality or unreality, and mediating between different events and scenes in order to create a sense of continuity.*

But in your suspense film, how do you figure out when to use music? Trying to teach how to use music in suspense sequences presents complications. Music is hard to quantify when it is married to visuals because that synergetic combination is specific to a scene or moment. The variety of possible combinations is endless—like fingerprints or snowflakes, each one is unique. On top of that, a modern movie like *The Bourne Identity* is filled with various moments ranging from subtle drums to brief orchestral interludes. It's often hard to figure out where music ends and where ambient sound design begins.

In my interview with *The Bourne Identity*'s editor Saar Klein, he says, "I hate watching a dramatic scene and hearing the music start at the beginning of the emotional moment to 'help it'; it doesn't help." He says, "Music placed in this manner takes me out of the moment and makes me feel manipulated." (See chapter 21 for the full interview.)

WHEN NOT TO USE MUSIC

Overall, suspense music follows a pretty easy rule of thumb: When the protagonist has to be quiet to hide from something, there should be no music. We should hear everything that they hear in real time. A music score will take us out of that moment.

Those "that was close!" moments that you created in previous chapters probably won't need music either.

Casual Hitchcock fans may point to the famous shower scene in *Psycho* (1960), but may be surprised to find out that most of his murder scenes contained no music. The shower scene in *Psycho* is the notable exception, and apparently he resisted using it there. Perhaps the presence of the iconic violin strums in the shower made the scene easier to watch, making it edge more toward fantasy rather than harsh reality.

That's what Hitchcock believed—that a music score evokes an element of fantasy, and therefore the absence of a score is more realistic (fig. 11.1).

FANTASY ⟵————————⟶ **REALITY**
(music) *(no music)*

Figure 11.1. Using a music score tends to bring the viewer into fantasy rather than stark reality.

When the viewer can clearly hear everything the protagonist hears, they are more easily able to feel they are sharing the moment in real time. They can put themselves fully into the scene. Any music score imposed into that is going to become a distraction from those sounds.

Interestingly, if you take a look at Hitchcock's very first sound film, *Blackmail* (1929), the murder scene didn't include a music score. With this silence, he was able to demonstrate that the policeman outside was unable to hear Alice's screams. He cuts to a view of the policeman happily walking down the street as Alice calls out. When the cop doesn't seem to notice, it creates a sense of anxious frustration that builds the suspense of the moment. We ask, "Why didn't the cop hear the screams?" That's a question that may have been lost with the presence of a score.

When a music score is present, our minds tend to stop listening for background details in the scene. Music transports our perception of events into a more emotional and abstract realm, and away from the stark realism of the scene. We are no longer purely present in the scene. The effect of this is that our feelings of suspense are dissipated.

Because of this, "that was close!" scenes in the Hitchcock world tend to have no music. These scenes, which are built surrounding a secret almost getting out, benefit from the cold, stark reality of silence. They mimic the biological response that we have in these situations—we breathe softly and swallow quietly in an attempt to hide our anxieties. We get very quiet behind the savanna grass when hiding from the hungry lion.

As an example, major "that was close!" moments in *North by Northwest* (1959) are all silent—as the protagonists share a hotel elevator with the antagonists, they hide from the police in the train station, the crop-duster scene where one protagonist faces the antagonist, and the auction scene. While all these moments are tense, they benefit from utilizing the ambient sounds of the setting to enhance tension. Once the suspense has been relieved, however, music kicks in.

Family Plot (1976) stops its suspenseful music for dramatic effect as Arthur walks into his office to find that Maloney has escaped through the window. As the camera pans to the open window, the music suddenly stops, emphasizing the emptiness of the room and the sound of the wind blowing the curtains. According to composer John Williams, who was still new to scoring at the time, he had written music over the entire window scene. Hitchcock taught him that silence was often more effective than music (Bouzereau).

WHEN TO USE MUSIC

If all of the key suspense scenes in your film are absent a score, when, then, should music be used? Music is good for opening sequences, journeys through geographic space, romantic encounters, and when any plot revelation causes a big shift in perspective for the audience. At least, that's what we can surmise from surveying the music used in Hitchcock's body of work. Here's a breakdown of common film moments that can benefit from music score.

OPENING SEQUENCE

Music in your opening scenes can help to establish both the mood for the film and the attitude of the director. The mood that Hitchcock often planted was playful, cartoonish, and flamboyant in order to evoke the teasing relationship between him and his audience. He also believed that scary, dramatic films should open as comedies so the audience will feel good before drama enters. Not only does this allow the drama to have more of an impact when it arrives, comedy helps the audience like the characters before something happens to them (Gottlieb, 1995).

BEGINNINGS OF SCENES

Subsequently, as the film plays out, openings to new scenes rarely need to use music to reestablish an existing mood. Hitchcock preferred to use ambient sound to begin a scene. This is especially true if the characters begin the scene leisurely, awaiting more tension to appear. But if a protagonist is nervously entering a new location, such as an ominous house on a hill, music can emote their feelings of anxiety.

MOVING THROUGH GEOGRAPHIC SPACE

Hitchcockian music is most prominent when the protagonist is in motion, traveling to a new location or running from a previous one. During these trips, often shown in montage or point-of view (see chapter 4), the music represents the forward action of the protagonist, as they change the story's progression. The protagonist has made a choice and set out on a path to change something, thus the music emulates that sense of adventure or nervous power play against the antagonist. Conversely, music helps embody the forward motions of the antagonist as well—think *Jaws* or *Star Wars*.

CHASE SCENES

Chase scenes are also packed with fast, anticipatory music, often grandiose and even playful. The busied, adventuristic music of *North by Northwest* (1959) by Bernard Herrmann is probably one of the most memorable scores of Hitchcock's body of work. It gives the chase scenes a feeling of cinematic, at times comic, grandeur. The music here is, again, an arm of the director's teasing attitude toward the audience. Rather than setting a predictable, ominous tone, the music is more about evoking this director/audience game. (See chapter 7.)

PLOT POINTS

As expected, major plot turns—such as the inciting incident—generally have a music score, usually mirroring the reactions of the protagonist to these shifting events. Sometimes, though, the music is more about the shift in perspective for the audience rather than the character on screen. Whenever time and space shifts in a film's transitions from one scene to another, music helps the viewer feel it, and this includes shifts in plot as well.

ACCENT A SURPRISE

Hitchcock would often use short bursts of horns to accent a surprise. Just after a surprising moment, the horns would punctuate the reaction shot. This style was very common in the early days of comedy, and Bernard Herrmann used it frequently in Hitchcock films as well. It is a reminder that comedy shares an important balance with tension. (See chapter 14.)

LOVE SCENES

Romantic scenes also include a music score to amplify the emotional connection being shared by the couple as they are falling in love and embrace. These love scenes are full of abstract, passionate emotion amplified through the music. With the presence of music, it brings us out of the reality of the scene and into a fantasy mode.

DIEGETIC MUSIC

Instead of a score, Hitchcock preferred to use diegetic music from within a location wherever possible—that is, music that is heard by the characters. Often this would be from a radio or record player in restaurants, hotel lobbies, dining cars of trains, and carnivals. Or the music could be coming from a live band in the restaurant, for example. Even though diegetic music is supposed to be part of the locale, it can be made to either emulate the mood of the characters in the scene or contrast with it.

Rear Window (1954) uses diegetic music almost in its entirety. Hitchcock cleverly built a struggling piano composer into the story, so that his practice sessions would provide the neighborhood with a score. This diegetic score, of course, was manipulated by Hitchcock to comment on the events.

In *North by Northwest* (1959), Hitchcock used the train whistle as a type of natural score to demarcate the passage of time between scenes and keep the tension alive.

Location music can also be used to contrast with a dramatic scene, where happy music accompanies a dreadful scene. Since Hitchcock loved to make light of dangerous situations, this was a way to avoid being obviously flamboyant with a music score and instead using the setting to do it organically. A scene in *The 39 Steps* (1935) is a clever example of this contrast. After gunshots are heard in an auditorium, the band is instructed to keep playing happy music to prevent a panic.

In Hitchcock's TV episodes "The Crystal Trench" (1959) and "Revenge" (1955), the settings include happy waltz music during some of the most ominous scenes. In "The Crystal Trench," Stella is being told about the death of her husband while the band is playing happy music in the background. She stares off into the distance in shock while the band keeps playing. It's almost as if the music is mocking her tragedy. A similar moment in "Revenge" puts happy music from a hotel lobby against a murder in one of the rooms upstairs.

> *Music serves as either a counterpoint or a comment on whatever scene is being played.*—ALFRED HITCHCOCK (Gottlieb 2003)

Partially, this ironic contrast was a way for Hitchcock to make it easier for his audiences to experience such traumatic events. He once said: We want to amuse them, not depress them (Gottlieb).

At the same time, using happy diegetic music during a murder scene is part of the teasing game that he plays with his audiences. It's a coy way for him to indicate that, once again, we are part of this practical joke that he's playing on us. This makes his presence as director in the story more active in our minds as we watch, and it provokes reflexivity. (See chapter 7.)

Plus, inappropriately fun music alerts the audience of the lonely, helplessness of the situation—that none of the bystanders have noticed the tragedy. Either they are so self-absorbed that they are unaware of their surroundings, or they simply don't care. This sense of helplessness is a key ingredient in the complex recipe of suspense.

DIALOGUE AS MUSIC

Human speech can be musical as well, and often Hitchcock treated dialogue as if it were music. Dialogue has always been something which Hitchcock treated as merely sounds emanating from the mouths of his characters, whereas the story was revealed visually in other ways—by a glance, a close-up on an object, a reaction, etc. Despite this visual emphasis, the speaking rhythms of the characters were very important. In fact, he would coach his actors on the emphasis of every line and every pause.

There is a fascinating transcript from one of Hitchcock's actor meetings with Tippi Hedren on *The Birds* (1963) that I encourage everyone to read through. It's published in Dan Auiler's *Hitchcock's Notebooks*, pp. 389–413. Among other things, it reveals Hitchcock's philosophy on dialogue. He treats dialogue like music, planning out every pause, hesitation, and where the pacing should slow down or speed up to crescendo. Some lines are acted less emotionally to create contrast with emotional ones, some whispered, some frantic. He coached Hedren on when to purse her lips, when to use the punch line of a joke to hide a change of subject, and other variations of rhythm and emphasis.

While actors shouldn't spend a lot of energy being self-conscious about their speech patterns, this transcript certainly provides an eye-opening look into the importance of this dance between facial expressions, speech, and hidden secrets.

SUGGESTED VIEWING

▲ *North by Northwest* (1959)—some versions of the DVD allow you to watch with a music-only audio track without dialogue.

FURTHER READING

Auiler, Dan 2001. *Hitchcock's Notebooks: An Authorized and Illustrated Look Inside the Creative Mind of Alfred Hitchcock*, Harper Collins, New York.

Bays, Jeffrey 2014. *Between the Scenes,* Michael Wiese Productions.

Bouzereau, Laurent 2001. *Plotting Family Plot*, documentary, Universal Studios Home Video.

Gorbman, C 1987. "Why Music? The Sound Film and its Spectator," in *Unheard Melodies,* Indiana University Press, Indianapolis, pp. 53–69.

Gottlieb, Sidney 1995. *Hitchcock on Hitchcock: Selected Writings and Interviews*, University of California Press, USA.

Gottlieb, Sidney 2003. *Alfred Hitchcock Interviews*, University Press of Mississippi, Jackson, p. 46.

Pallasmaa, J 2001. *The Architecture of Image: Existential Space in Cinema*, Rakennustieto, Helsinki, p.119.

Smith, Jeff 1999. "Movie Music as Moving Music: Emotion, Cognition, and the Film Score," in *Passionate Views: Film, Cognition, and Emotion,* Ed. Carl Plantinga and Greg Smith, John Hopkins University Press, Baltimore and London, pp. 147–167.

Truffaut, François 1986. *Hitchcock / Truffaut with the collaboration of Helen G. Scott*, Paladin, London, p. 222.

SUSPENSE MYTH NO. 4

SUSPENSE IS BUILT BY A MUSICAL SCORE

Perhaps surprisingly, Hitch believed that music only got in the way of tense moments of crisis. It is no coincidence that with his first sound film, *Blackmail*, he pioneered the use of silence as a dramatic device: By keeping that film's murder scene sans score, he accentuated the fact that the victim's screams go unheard.

A lack of music brings foreboding reality to the forefront. You hear everything the characters hear—every footstep, every creak. The small details of background become part of the tension, bringing you closer into the moment.

Hitch made entire films without musical scores (*The Birds* is a famous example) and most of his murder scenes were music-less. He tended to use music in the more comedic parts of his films, but once a crisis breaks out, music disappears in favor of stark realism. ◢

CHAPTER 12

INNER THOUGHTS ALOUD

What is it? Why is everything so fuzzy? It's like, like dust on my eyes. How could that be? Hey, I can't close them. I can't, I can't move. Anything. I can't feel. I'm paralyzed. But maybe, maybe if I concentrate. No. No, it won't work. I can't move. I'm. Wait a minute. Wait a minute now. It won't do any good to get in a sweat. I'm alive at least.

THOSE ARE THE INNER THOUGHTS of William Callew (played by Joseph Cotten) in Hitchcock's TV episode "Breakdown" (1955), heard clearly via voice-over.

When your protagonist must remain quiet, or is unable to speak, an effective tool is to reveal their inner thought process in real time through a stream of consciousness voice-over. We hear a live rendition of their random thoughts as the scene plays out, often with a slight echo effect to indicate that it is not heard by anyone else. This immediately makes the character's presence subjective in a way not possible with pure visuals.

A contemporary example of this is on an episode of the TV show *Seinfeld* when Elaine (Julia Louis-Dreyfus) is standing on a subway train among a crowd of New Yorkers. The lights go off and we hear her thoughts giving commentary on the situation, revealing her wishes, fears, and opinions of the people around her. In this instance, it is used for comic effect, but directors like Hitchcock have been able to prove its power in a dramatic context, as in the above example in "Breakdown."

Hitchcock's use of the stream of consciousness voice-over was a lot more prevalent in his TV works, but he did use it on occasion in his feature films. *Psycho* (1960), for example, uses a version of these inner thoughts while Marion Crane is driving with the stolen money. She imagines the voices of other people talking about her.

Since *Alfred Hitchcock Presents*—and the spinoff series *Suspicion*—utilized a lot of writers from radio, like Francis Cockrell, this technique naturally came with the territory. It may be that Hitchcock viewed TV as a more personal and intimate medium than cinema, where the viewer is watching on a small screen in the privacy of their living room. Whatever the reason, stream of consciousness is common in his twenty works of TV, like "The Case of Mr. Pelham," "Mr. Blanchard's Secret," "Four O'Clock," "Dip in the Pool," and the aforementioned "Breakdown."

THE ULTIMATE IN SUBJECTIVITY

The beauty of the stream of consciousness technique is that when the voice-over is added to a shot of the actor's face, it provides instant access to the character's thoughts. It allows an unfettered evaluation of their logic, their plans, and their perceived roadblocks and consequences to achieving those plans.

It also has the effect of speaking aloud the audience's thought process while watching a film. You can easily imagine that a person watching this scene from "Four O'Clock" (1957) would be thinking in very much the same way as Paul when he hears the gas man pull up outside:

> That's right out front I think. Across the street. Yes. It's a man. Sounds like a man. He's coming in. Come on. Come on in. It's not locked. Oh no. Those two kids must have locked it after they tied me up. They slipped the catch. Why did they have to leave? Why couldn't she be here. The one man who

would have to bring her down that would be sure to see me. Why don't they come back? Come back. They could still come back. Drive up in front right now. He'd see them, he'd wait. There's still time. Oh Fran. Come back, come back. Please do. Drive up in front and stop. He'll get out and make you let him in. Please come home. Please come now. You can save me. Don't you see it's the only way—it's the only way I can live.

Paul is tied up and gagged in the basement, desperate for the gas man to see him. His inner thoughts drive the suspense and urgency of the scene, and emote his desperation for his wife to come home and open the door for the gas man. Since it's very similar to what the audience is thinking, it allows the connection between viewer and protagonist to grow stronger.

During the above narration we see the gas man's shadow through the window, approaching the door. As the man gives up and walks away, we feel the same helplessness Paul does. If only the gas man would find out. It provokes the audience to want to step in and interfere, if only we had that power.

CAMERA TREATMENT TO MATCH

What do you do with the camera while the voice-over is playing? In "Four O'Clock," Hitchcock uses a few tracking shots around Paul's face to make it aesthetically dynamic while the voice narrates. The scenes are cut normally with point-of-view sequences to display the progression of the scene from Paul's perspective. Essentially, Paul is framed and treated as if he's actually speaking. The only difference being an emphasis on his eyes, which have sole emotive power in the shot.

A TV episode like "Breakdown," on the other hand, is more complicated because William cannot move his eyes at all. His state of paralysis negates any usage of true point-of-view or emotive eyes for any length of time, as William is permanently staring into the sky at a fixed position.

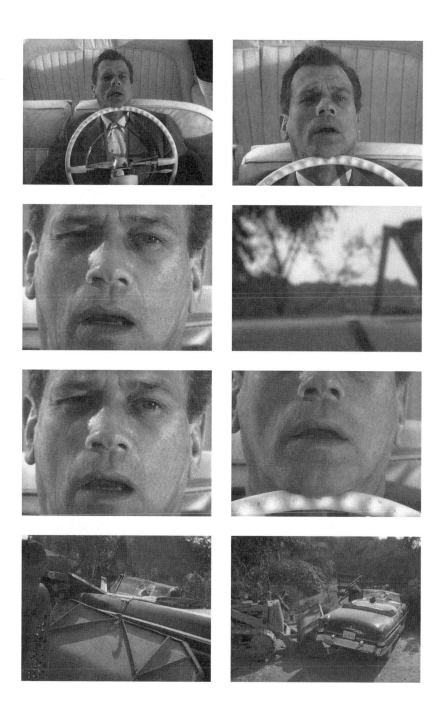

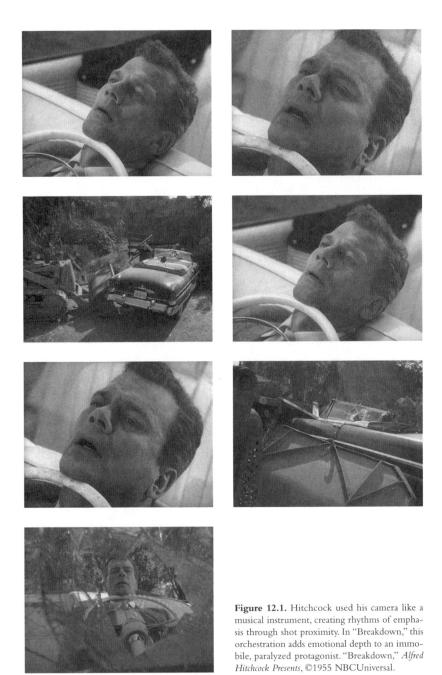

Figure 12.1. Hitchcock used his camera like a musical instrument, creating rhythms of emphasis through shot proximity. In "Breakdown," this orchestration adds emotional depth to an immobile, paralyzed protagonist. "Breakdown," *Alfred Hitchcock Presents*, ©1955 NBCUniversal.

"Breakdown" shows Hitchcock experimenting with camera orchestration (see chapter 6), compiling various distances and angles from William's face. For a scene that is about a motionless man in an unmoving surrounding, it is a highly creative camera treatment that calls upon the subjective nature of the voice-over.

What we find is that wide shots are used when the voice-over gets vague, but extreme close-ups are saved for those lines of dialogue that make an important point. He even uses extreme close-ups of William's mouth as his thoughts become panicked. When William considers his surroundings, Hitchcock cuts back to wide shots of the scene.

The choice of angles Hitchcock uses are quite varied, fragmenting the scene from all perspectives and distances (fig. 12.1). Sometimes we see William from the side, sometimes from behind, from below, and even from above. This resulting montage is reminiscent of a Picasso cubist painting, where various perspectives of the subject are cut and diced abstractly onto the flat canvas.

SUGGESTED VIEWING

▲ *Alfred Hitchcock Presents*, "Breakdown," Season 1, Episode 7 (1955)—an entire episode using the stream-of-consciousness narration technique.

▲ *Suspicion*, "Four O'Clock," Season 1, Episode 1 (1957)—We hear Paul's inner thoughts through much of the film.

▲ *Seinfeld*, "The Subway," Season 3, Episode 13 (1992)—Elaine's thoughts are heard aloud while she is standing on the subway.

PART FIVE
SHARPEN THE CLARITY

CHAPTER 13

CARVING A CLEAR PATH OF AUDIENCE BELIEF

SUSPENSE REQUIRES AN ABSOLUTE, unquestionable clarity of understanding of the events on screen. As the trusted storyteller, you must make the story easy for the viewer to grasp every step of the way. Clarity forces the events to become potent and hyper-present. It gives you that raw emotional investment that keeps your viewers hanging on for more.

> *What is drama, after all, but life with the dull bits cut out.*—ALFRED HITCHCOCK (Truffaut)

We've all at some time in our lives had to endure a bad storyteller—someone that rambles, talks in riddles, or never reaches the point.

The first thing clarity does is get everyone on the same page. Often our perception of a story is based on our mood at the time. Psychological studies have shown that audiences who watch a movie actually emulate the emotions of the movie. Where individuals may all be in different moods going in, by the end of the movie everyone is feeling the same way. As the storyteller you want this unification to happen as early as possible. With clarity, everyone is in sync and feels and experiences the movie in the same way, rather than just casually dipping in and out of interest.

Secondly, clarity removes boredom. When a storyteller creates a narrative that is too difficult to understand or relate to, they force the audience into mental fatigue. Make the audience struggle to think and they'll switch off. Hitchcock said, "You can't have blurred thinking in suspense" (Bogdanovich).

BINARY OPPOSITIONS

For centuries the great storytellers knew that opposites make things easier to understand. Think about a chessboard. Because the squares of the chessboard are alternated white and black, it's easy to determine at a glance where each player can move. A solid white chess board would be hard to follow. Entirely white pieces on a white board would be a disaster!

This means: No two characters should look alike. Make use of different hair colors. And no similar-looking characters should dress alike. If two men of the same height and age are wearing the exact same color suit, the audience is going to get confused. You don't want them struggling to keep track of characters—this will eat up all their mental energy (Gottlieb).

If all your female characters are blondes with the exact same makeup style and the same voice—they might as well be one character. Half of your audience might be able to keep track, but the other half will not.

> One of the fatal things in suspense is to have a mind that is confused. If the audience is confused they won't emote. Clarify, clarify, clarify.—ALFRED HITCHCOCK (Bogdanovich)

This goes for location choices from one scene to the next, too. Locations should be starkly different (see my book *Between the Scenes* for more on this.) Audiences tend to compartmentalize the story based on the location of each scene, so make sure the geography of your film is changing and progressing, painting an easy mental map to follow.

SIMPLICITY OF THINKING

Even if you have a complex, intellectual story where the characters are entwined in an elaborate conspiracy, you should shift the focus of the storytelling toward the simplistic in order for suspense to be felt.

The easiest way to simplify a scene is to turn the focus to suspense objects. Suspense objects are objects in a scene that are followed by the camera (see chapter 5). They have the advantage of being visual, and therefore can provoke the audience's memory quite easily. The audience can easily track where the objects are and anticipate how they will affect the story when they're moved around.

This is a lot like computer adventure games of the 1990s, putting the game player into a setting and waiting for them to look for clues. The player clicks every object they find in the scene and can either "look" at it to get more information about it, or "grab" it to use it for later. Soon the player may be able to combine two objects they collected into a tool which can be useful to advance the story. Or, the player may be able to give the object to another character in order to develop trust. In the game environment, objects become a way for the player to interact with the narrative.

Similarly, in your movie, objects can bring the viewer closer into your narrative, making them feel like they can affect the story. While they can't actually affect the story, they can feel on the verge of being able to do so. This makes them more susceptible to suspense.

Pare your complex cerebral story down into simple objects. When this isn't possible, find a trivial subject of focus in the scene rather than the dramatic. (See more in chapter 15.)

CLEAR PATH OF BELIEF

Not only should your plot be clear, present, and simple, the viewer should be led along a path of belief about what's happening at every moment. It's almost like structuring a maze for a mouse. Your plot can zigzag, include dead ends and red herrings, but there should be only one exit.

Being clear doesn't necessarily mean being honest. You can mislead the audience on purpose, take them on wild goose chases, and play on their skepticism.

Because you've grabbed strict control over the material and made it simple and easy to follow, you can trick the audience into believing a certain reality about the story. Then you can build in a skeptical character to make us question that reality. You can also change that reality at any time.

Take the example of Hitchcock's TV episode "Mr. Blanchard's Secret" (1956), which we examine in my *Hitch20* docu-series. Babs has created a conspiracy theory about the neighbor being missing or dead. We follow her logic until it is temporarily disproven—the neighbor shows up at the door, alive. The conspiracy changes from being murdered to being hidden; the husband keeps her locked up at home because he's embarrassed by her. Then this is disproven. The conspiracy changes again, and we follow along her theory that the neighbor is a kleptomaniac and has stolen a vase.

What makes this entertaining is that the viewer is constantly falling for it. We're led into the fiction, and then we see it isn't true. Each time we realize we've been fooled, we're still ready to believe the next conspiracy. Hitchcock's clear path makes us need the conspiracy to be true in order to find closure on the story.

REALITY BAROMETER & SKEPTIC

With a story that plays along the boundary between reality and fiction like "Blanchard," the audience is constantly shifting belief between the two. A supporting skeptical character is a good way to help ground the audience and keep them wondering. This skeptical character serves as a reality barometer, because they help us determine what is real in this story-world.

We know that the movie we're watching is fiction, but we want to be lured into a suspension of disbelief. We want to believe it's all real. So it is useful to have a character that helps us gauge this level of reality.

In "Blanchard," the husband John is the reality barometer. He is so accustomed to Babs's wild conspiracy theories that he ignores them. In fact, he is so excessively bored and uninterested that we prefer not to believe him.

In Hitchcock's *Rear Window* (1954), Detective Doyle is the reality barometer. He's always there with the facts to debunk the latest conspiracy. The characters feel they must convince him, and that makes the pursuit of truth that much more interesting and emotionally rewarding.

Hitchcock's TV episode "The Case of Mr. Pelham" is also about a paranoid character that believes he has a doppelgänger trying to take over his identity. The psychologist is the reality barometer, serving as a skeptic to warn us that this guy might be crazy. Hitchcock shows us suspense objects that convince us the psychologist is wrong.

In Dan Trachtenberg's *10 Cloverfield Lane* (2016), the protagonist is actually the reality barometer and the antagonists have the conspiracy. Howard and Emmett have convinced Michelle that an environmental disaster prevents them from leaving the bunker. We closely follow Michelle's path of evidence and believe her skepticism, until it is disproven. Each time her skepticism is disproven, we trust Howard until the next round.

The ironic effect of having this skeptical character is that it tends to solidify our belief in the conspiracy. It's basic human nature to believe gossip. Sometimes we want to believe it even when the facts get in the way. We look for the next piece of evidence that rebukes Michelle's skepticism, and we get a sense of relief that she's wrong. We want to believe the conspiracy, and the skeptic is just a persistent obstacle that provokes us into solidifying our allegiances.

So it's important to construct a clear path through the maze for the audience at all times. Know what the audience should think at every moment, and make sure there are concrete "walls" in the maze to guide them, via suspense objects and reality barometers. Leave no vague areas where the audience isn't really sure what's going on. Keep it all simple, streamline it so the mouse will be easily lured on its way to the cheese.

CLARITY IN "THE BOURNE IDENTITY"

In Doug Liman's *The Bourne Identity* (2002), the audience knows exactly what's going on at all times, yet is kept just as alert and paranoid as the characters are. It's a great example of suspense, tension, and clarity. The film pits protagonist and antagonist against each other (Jason Bourne vs. the CIA) in a cat-and-mouse game until the conflict finally comes to a head.

Jason (Matt Damon) wakes up on a rescue boat with amnesia, and begins his quest to find out who he is. After winning a few instinctually provoked battles with the police, he realizes he has special combat training. Meanwhile, the audience is made aware of the CIA operation bent on capturing him.

Bourne Identity is a mix of hiding in various apartments, hotels, and houses, with chase scenes through the streets of Paris. Once the CIA finds out where he's been, Bourne is always a few steps ahead of them. Each time Jason gains another clue about who he is, he gets closer to realizing the immorality of what he's been trained to do until the final standoff, where he fully regains his memories.

Suspense in *Bourne Identity* is built around hiding and the fear of getting caught. We quickly learn that his antagonists can pop up out of nowhere, so the invisible danger keeps us on our toes. The key to *Bourne Identity* is that the audience knows who Bourne is well before he figures it out. So the closer he gets to facing his CIA handlers, the higher the suspense for us.

Tension in *Bourne* is wound up tight through the use of silence and omnipresent ambient sounds—placing us in the moment. Tension is skillfully released with moments of calm and contemplation, so that we are recharged for the next round of tension.

You'll also notice that each actor cast in the movie is easily distinguishable within the narrative. They are of varying ages and races, with different hair colors and clothing styles. Each time a recurring character pops on the screen we can easily ascertain at a glance who it is without confusion. Bourne is a clean-cut, athletic blond, and never goes up against anyone with that description.

Each time Bourne finds new evidence of his identity, we clearly see it in a close-up shot—the computer chip, the stash of money, passports, the gun, the "wanted" notice, the marksman's phone. We are provoked to track this evidence and believe the mystery he is uncovering based on the physicality of these objects.

The reality barometer character in *Bourne* is the girl, Marie, who gets swept up in the adventure. She plays the role of skeptic. At a restaurant, she tries to talk him out of his paranoia, but we soon learn his fear was justified. In another key scene, they are relaxing in his apartment when an agent crashes through the window and begins shooting. This scene is so traumatic that she vomits on the way out of the building.

Marie's reactions confirm the craziness of the situation contrasted with Bourne's calmness. She becomes a way for the audience to experience emotional reaction, since Bourne is a stoic superhero, always in control and unable to express his fear. When she realizes that Bourne is a CIA marksman, she begins to fear him. She later becomes a counterbalance for her cousin's overreaction to the attack on his home. Marie is essentially an audience advocate, or surrogate. Our questions and reactions are embodied within her character.

Clarity is an important part of making those close-call moments around the secrets you've planted much more intense. With clearly demarcated locations, and an easily distinguishable cast of characters, your film will be easy to follow. By simplifying the plot into universal instincts and visual objects, everyone in the room will be unquestionably tuned in. When everyone in your audience is synchronized into the same mindset while watching your film, the greater their enjoyment.

SUGGESTED VIEWING

Watch these films and TV episodes mentioned in this chapter to learn more about carving a clear path of audience belief.

- ▲ *Alfred Hitchcock Presents*, "Mr. Blanchard's Secret," Season 2, Episode 13 (1956)
- ▲ *Rear Window* (1954)—paranoid story with a reality barometer.
- ▲ *Alfred Hitchcock Presents*, "The Case of Mr. Pelham," Season 1, Episode 10 (1955)
- ▲ *Offing David* (2008), Dir. Jeffrey Michael Bays—simplicity in lieu of deep drama.
- ▲ *The Bourne Identity* (2002), Dir. Doug Liman.

FURTHER READING

Bays, Jeffrey 2014. *Between the Scenes*, Michael Wiese Productions.
Bays, Jeffrey 2014–17. *Hitch20*, web-series, YouTube.
Bogdanovich, Peter 1997. *Who the Devil Made It*, Ballantine Books, New York.
Gottlieb, Sidney 2003. *Alfred Hitchcock Interviews*, University Press Mississippi, Jackson.
Truffaut, François 1986. *Hitchcock / Truffaut with the collaboration of Helen G. Scott*, Paladin, London.

SUSPENSE MYTH NO. 5

KEEP INFORMATION FROM THE AUDIENCE AND THEY'LL FEEL SUSPENSE

Wrong. In order to create the Hitchcockian brand of suspense, you must create a situation where the audience knows clearly what's going to happen, but is helpless to stop it. To do this, your audience must know more than the characters do. This is the director's famous Bomb Theory, in which the audience knows the proverbial bomb is under the table, going off in five minutes, while characters carry on with triviality, completely unaware. By playing on the viewer's empathy, you generate a visceral interest in the success of the characters' plans.

This doesn't mean you can't trick your audience. By all means, lead them down the wrong path and then surprise them with a twist. As long as they feel the clarity of danger unfolding, they'll love you for it. ◢

CHAPTER 14

CLARITY WITH TENSION & LAUGHS

IN THE PREVIOUS CHAPTER, you learned how to clarify the elements of your film in order to keep the audience's full attention. Making things easy to follow and understand will in turn increase their susceptibility to suspense. Tension is another way to sharpen the audience's focus and prevent daydreaming and wandering boredom.

First, you'll need to have your close-call scenarios in place. Let's summarize the goal: You want to plant a secret within your story-world, and then build in some "that was close!" moments to tease the audience about that secret getting out.

Tension is different from suspense because it is more present in the moment. It's the beat by beat feeling of intensity as a sequence builds toward a crescendo. Tension can increase the suspense of those close-call moments in two primary ways:

- By intensifying the details of the scene
- By creating frustration in the audience by delaying the impending outcome

You force the viewer to concentrate their attention by either putting it all in their face, or by trying to distract them with something else. These techniques increase their feeling of suspense and their anticipation toward the resolution.

Think of it like a roller coaster. Each steep dive and fast curve is balanced by the delayed inclines and straight track. A good roller coaster strikes a perfect balance for an enjoyable ride.

INTENSITY OF DETAIL

Tension is a way of sharpening the attention of the audience and forcing them to focus on details. You make the details jump out at them. It's one thing that causes them to feel present in the moment. This is done though the audiovisual artifice: camera, editing, sound design, music, etc.

HEIGHTENING VISUALS & SOUNDS

Shifting toward close-ups on faces and objects puts those details in the forefront. Using close-ups with fragmented framing, along with quick edits can increase tension. Silence accompanied by crisp, specific sounds also increases audience focus. Music takes the viewer out of the reality of the scene, so leave it out during tense moments (see chapter 11). This allows the audience to focus on sounds that the protagonist hears. You can intensify these sounds by making them extra loud and crisp, only emphasizing those specific sounds that help sharpen the clarity of the scene.

PROCEDURAL DETAILS

Once you have your suspense scenario in motion, it increases tension to spend extra screen time with one of the characters carrying out a specific, often mundane, task. It works for four reasons:

1. It prolongs the impending outcome.
2. It adds dramatic weight, sometimes ironically, to the task being done.
3. It focuses the audience's concentration, thus increasing tension.
4. There's a threat that if it goes wrong, it will ruin the desired outcome.

Take, for instance, the Hitchcock TV episode "Poison" (1958), where Harry is trapped in his bed by a poisonous snake under the sheets. A doctor is called in and decides to perform a delicate procedure to sedate the snake. First he must carefully position a tube and funnel under the sheets. Then he takes out a chemical and pours it into the funnel. The more screen time spent watching each detail of this flimsy procedure increases the tension of the dangerous moment.

OBJECTS OF PARANOIA

You can also make the details jump out when the protagonist is in a heightened state of anxiety and begins feeling paranoid about his surroundings. In "Four O'Clock," Paul thinks his wife has been cheating on him by having a man over to the house during the day. When Paul sees extra food missing in the refrigerator and extra cigarette butts in the ashtray, he thinks this all adds up to support his suspicion. Focusing on these objects increases his anxiety, and ours.

STREAM OF CONSCIOUSNESS

As shown in chapter 12, making the audience feel present in the moment may also include access to the inner thoughts of the protagonist. You can use voice-over to bring alive the character's thoughts in real time as they react in a stream-of-consciousness narration while the scene plays out. Allowing your audience to hear the thoughts of the protagonist allows them to follow his logic, fears, and conspiracy theories. It is a level of moment-by-moment detail unmatched by anything else.

COMICAL DELAYS

The second way tension can be used to increase suspense is by creating playful frustration in the audience. Frustration is created by interrupting and delaying the impending outcome, causing the audience to hang on in anticipation. Frustration sharpens audience focus, because the viewer has to work harder to avoid being distracted. Comedy is the key to making this work, because it helps make the frustration more enjoyable.

Let's explore some ways you can generate this enjoyable frustration in the viewer, primarily through characters that nonchalantly impede the progress of the story.

MALFUNCTIONS & INCOMPETENCE

It's probably the most fun aspect of increasing tension—using supporting characters in a comedic way to frustrate the outcome. In the Hitchcock world, people make mistakes and are lazy about their jobs during moments when their actions are most needed.

Police, detectives, and essentially anyone of expertise are much funnier when they aren't very good at their job. Even better, they really don't want to do their job and think of any excuse to avoid it. This irony not only makes them human and endearing, it fuels that dual roller coaster of laughs and screams. Their incompetence at a time when the story needs them the most creates an anxious frustration in the audience that builds tension. It's your choice if they finally see the light and redeem themselves in the end. Either way, it adds to the unpredictable world of suspense.

In Hitchcock's TV episode "Bang! You're Dead" (1961), suspense is built around Jackie's mother trying to warn people at the supermarket that her son is lost with a loaded gun. She tries to interrupt a stock clerk in an argument with a dissatisfied customer, but the clerk won't listen. She tries to tell management to send out an announcement over the store's PA system, but she's interrupted there, too. When she finally makes the announcement herself, a loud coffeemaker interrupts the message. Each attempt at trying to get the word out fails because the supermarket staff is too busy to pay attention to her. As the audience, we find this both frustrating and amusing as tension rises.

MISUNDERSTOOD FACTS

This one is also true in real life. During a crisis, people tend to get frantic and make dumb mistakes or clerical errors. Very often in a Hitchcock movie, someone will get a phone number wrong, or misunderstand a name for a place, or the protagonist sees conspiracy where there is none. All of these are things that the audience could correct, if only they could communicate with those fools on the screen—the delightful frustration that makes suspense so entertaining.

CHARACTERS NOT IN THE KNOW

When a supporting character doesn't know the hidden secret, it's a great opportunity for them to tease the audience with their ignorance. Overemphasize their ignorance by putting them ever so close to stumbling upon the secret.

Very often this can occur in conversation, where the not-in-the-know character coincidentally begins talking about something very similar to the secret in the scene. This pushes the protagonist to hide their feelings of guilt, while the ignorant character ignores the obvious signs of their anxiety. Or, perhaps the protagonist becomes overly arrogant and flamboyant about the topic as a way of compensating and covering their guilt. All of this adds fuel to the tension in the scene.

COMEDY & TENSION WORKING TOGETHER

> *In the mystery and suspense genre, a tongue-in-cheek approach is indispensable.*—ALFRED HITCHCOCK (Truffaut)

As may already be clear, suspense is hardly possible without an element of comedy woven into the tension. The reason for this is that the viewer must enjoy the ride and feel safe. The viewer must trust that the director is not going to harm the audience, or put them through trauma. It's the same as with a roller coaster. When designing a roller coaster there is a limit to the amount of G-forces you can include so that the kids will still be giggling and gossiping about it when the ride rolls to a stop. Make it too dangerous and they'll never come back (Wheldon).

Just like that tickling feeling in your stomach when going down the first steep dive, comedy is a crucial part of making the ride of suspense successful. Just like those rubbery hands reaching out at your legs in the carnival haunted house, you giggle and playfully scream because you know it's not a real danger. When watching a scary film, you know it's not real. You must know you're not watching a real murder, or seeing real tragedy, because otherwise you won't enjoy the experience.

Even though Hitchcock was always branded as the Master of Suspense, he was equally a master of humor. The best of his works have struck a perfect balance between laughs and anxiety. The two sensations played off each other, so that during a suspense sequence you could go either way—you're nervous in the moment, but also amused that the director was so clever in setting up this moment. Very few filmmakers have been able to match that skill.

> My goal is to amuse the public and not to depress them. Going to the movies is like going to a restaurant. A film must satisfy body and mind.—ALFRED HITCHCOCK (Gottlieb)

Hitchcock used the perfect anecdote to explain this to Dick Cavett in 1972. He said there's a "fine line between tragedy and comedy" and he goes on to describe a man walking down the street reading a newspaper. The man is dressed prim and proper, with a top hat as a symbol of high dignity. He doesn't realize that he's walking toward an open manhole and suddenly falls down the hole. If this was in a film it would evoke laughter in the audience. But, the man might actually be hurt—that's the tragedy.

Figure 14.1. Comedy and tragedy are closely related.

UNPREDICTABLE CHARACTERS

Another key element of tension is unpredictability. In designing a cast of characters for a suspense ride they must first break the cliché from assumed archetypes. They should be surprising in their moral philosophy and make unpredictable decisions. And of course they should be capable of making dumb mistakes in the heat of the moment. You want your audience to be hanging on to every moment in awe of what your characters are doing.

Hitchcock's TV episode "Wet Saturday" is a great study for this type of broad casting that edges into the absurd. The story revolves around a family having a playful discussion about how to hide a death caused by their daughter. The conversation is nonchalant, as if it's no big deal. The teenage daughter has killed someone and the father doesn't want it to get out and harm the family's reputation. They treat the death as a fender bender—just a minor inconvenience that can be easily buffed out and forgotten.

So these characters concoct a cover story, which hinges on the crazy daughter's ability to keep quiet when the police arrive. But she has already been lurching around, wild-eyed, clearly not capable of staying calm. The resulting suspense revolves around this wacky daughter on the verge of being provoked into spilling the beans. Plus, an innocent friend arrives and gets roped into the conspiracy. Will he remain silent?

"Wet Saturday" is full of threats with shotguns, wooden mallets, dragging a dead body around, and the kicker: they push the body down the storm drain in the garage. It's a true comedy of the absurd, and at no point can anyone predict what these characters are capable of doing next. This setup is ripe for jaw-dropping suspense.

Now that you've explored ways to sharpen the clarity of your film through tension and frustrated laughter, let's turn back to a focus on objects that propel the visual story. In the next chapter we'll explore various ways suspense objects can be used to increase suspense.

SUGGESTED VIEWING

▲ *Suspicion*, "Four O'Clock," Season 1, Episode 1 (1957)
▲ *Alfred Hitchcock Presents*, "Lamb to the Slaughter," Season 3, Episode 28 (1958)
▲ *Alfred Hitchcock Presents*, "Wet Saturday," Season 2, Episode 1 (1956)

FURTHER READING

Auiler, Dan 2001. *Hitchcock's Notebooks: An Authorized and Illustrated Look Inside the Creative Mind of Alfred Hitchcock*, Harper Collins, New York—p. 102.

Bays, Jeffrey 2014–17. *Hitch20*, web-series, YouTube.

Cavett, Dick 1972. *The Dick Cavett Show*, ABC.

Gottlieb, Sidney 2003. *Alfred Hitchcock Interviews*, University Press Mississippi, Jackson—p. 126.

Wheldon, Huw 1964. "Huw Wheldon Meets Alfred Hitchcock," *Monitor*, May 5, 1964.

CHAPTER 15
SUSPENSE OBJECTS

STREAMLINING AND CLARITY help the audience fall easily into your film and get pulled along. Tension helps focus their attention. In an effort to simplify things, you should always think about how your complex intellectual and psychological ideas can be converted into a visual form, so that these important parts of your story are not just articulated in dialogue.

As mentioned in chapter 13, a good rule of thumb is to pare down your story into simple objects, or suspense objects. Objects like keys, necklaces, scarves, phones, ties, handwritten notes, receipts, tickets, etc., become important parts of the story's progression. They become physical evidence in the story's world that hands can interact with and eyes can react to. Objects simplify the story parts into easily followed items that hold meaning.

Suspense objects don't readily reveal their significance to unsuspecting characters, and thus easily tie into your hidden secrets and close-call scenarios. Who cares about a mink coat unless it matters to a person with a specific hidden secret about the coat ("Mrs. Bixby and the Colonel's Coat"). The criminals don't realize what "R.O.T." stands for on the matchbook in *North by Northwest*, but Eve does. We feel suspense, hoping that she notices and realizes that Thornhill is hiding in the house.

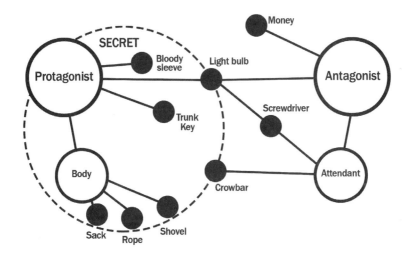

Figure 15.1. Objects in "One More Mile to Go" become the means for telling a visual story. The protagonist has objects that hide his secret murder, and the antagonists use objects that create close calls to that secret getting exposed.

Some of the objects are direct evidence in a crime, like the rope in *Rope* (1948), the scissors in *Dial M for Murder* (1954), or the lighter in *Strangers on a Train* (1951). These objects automatically hold power because their discovery can convict the protagonist and put an end to the story. (These are also MacGuffins. See chapter 16.)

Other suspense objects may merely be peripheral distractions in a sequence that are either red herrings or excuses for a character to do something. The loose closet door in *The Trouble With Harry* (1955) is an example of this, purely a red herring. Rupert's hat which he leaves behind in *Rope* (1948) causes him to return—an excuse to get him back into the apartment and continue the story.

In my film *Offing David* (2008), the two criminals, Adam and Matt, don't notice that the phone has fallen out of David's pocket during the murder, leaving it free to be discovered at any point. I built in many close-call scenarios as people find the phone and get closer to realizing that it belongs to David—something that would inevitably lead to the discovery that he's been killed.

Dan Trachtenberg, director of *10 Cloverfield Lane*, likens the use of suspense objects to a computer game. Puzzle or adventure games use objects as a way for the player to interact and advance the story. One object may be able to be combined with another, creating a new tool to be used on a character, or to escape, etc. Much of *10 Cloverfield Lane* features Michelle collecting objects and building various means of escape. (See our full interview with Trachtenberg in chapter 22.)

Let's take a look at the objects in Hitchcock's TV episode "One More Mile to Go" (1957). See the schematic in figure 15.1.

First, the objects that relate to the protagonist are things that could give away the secret if they are revealed:

▲ Sack—holds the body
▲ Rope—ties around the sack to keep it secure
▲ Shovel—to dig a hole for the body
▲ Trunk key—hidden as an excuse not to open trunk when cop is around
▲ Bloody sleeve—must also be hidden from cop's view

Next, the objects that relate to the antagonist (policeman and gas station attendant). These objects generate close calls.

▲ Light bulb—must be fixed, reason for cop to pull him over
▲ Screwdriver—to fix the light bulb
▲ Crowbar—to pry open the trunk
▲ Money—reason for cop to pull him over again

All of these objects provide visual icons that anchor the cinematic suspense. That is, suspense created through visuals on a movie screen relies on these objects because emphasizing them in close-ups is easily understood.

EVOKING THE TRIVIAL

As discussed in the previous chapter, comedy is an essential ingredient to make tension entertaining rather than annoying. Objects can be used to trivialize a traumatic situation and make it more comical. Hitchcock referred to this as "understatement."

By turning the focus of the tension away from the actual secret and toward a trivial object, it becomes much more entertaining (and therefore more gripping) for the audience. Essentially, it's a way of breaking away from the expected scenario.

Back to "One More Mile to Go." Here's the basic setup: A man has killed his wife and hidden the body in the trunk of his car. Now he's driving down the highway and gets pulled over by a policeman. What's the most obvious suspense question in this scene? *Will the policeman find the body?*

As the filmmaker, how do you build tension throughout this sequence? You need to find a reason for the policeman to open the trunk and find the body. The most obvious way would be for the police to already know about the missing woman and to have a reason to suspect the man. As the policeman pulls him over, tension is generated around his nervous reactions trying to hide what the police already suspect.

That's too obvious for Hitchcock, though. Rather than building tension around the body and the police's suspicions, he found it much more fun for the police to have no idea about the missing woman at all. He found a trivial object connected to the body only by circumstance. Hitchcock used the car's faulty taillight as a proxy suspense object.

A proxy suspense object is an object that stands in for something bigger. If you take a look at figure 15.1 you'll notice that the light bulb is the central object between the protagonist and antagonist. It generates the on-screen tension instead of the body in the trunk.

This light bulb creates a dance around the risk of getting caught. The policeman has pulled him over because of this burnt-out light and insists that the man immediately go to a gas station to replace it. The man resists and makes empty promises, until the cop pressures him to do so. They both drive to the gas station and the policeman waits as the gas station attendant replaces the light bulb.

Tension builds as the attendant meticulously screws in the new bulb. Hitchcock draws out every detail of this procedure, as the policeman takes a drink from a water fountain and watches from afar. The man waits nervously. By building tension around the bulb, we allow the audience to anticipate a new suspense question: Will they be able to fix this light? The comic obsession about the bulb allows us to enjoy the tension, making light of the life and death seriousness of the situation.

The "that was close!" scenario is still about whether the body will be discovered, but the light bulb is a way of drawing it out. Fixing the light relieves the close call.

When the new light bulb doesn't work either, Hitchcock then does everything possible to tease the audience about the cop's ignorance. The cop sits on the trunk. He rocks the car up and down to jar the light bulb. We imagine the dead body bouncing around in the trunk. Then he has the brilliant idea that a wire in the trunk must be loose, so he insists on opening the trunk. Tension rises.

The nervous man comes up with an excuse not to open the trunk. He pretends not to have the key. He detaches the trunk key (another suspense object, fig. 15.1) from his chain and hides it in his pocket. We see this in a close-up and then the man's face. The cop then suggests using a crowbar (fig. 15.1) to pry open the trunk. The man refuses as it might cause damage—why damage a trunk over a little light bulb?

The dance between the cop and nervous man continues, until finally the light comes on, saving the day. The man pays the attendant and drives away hurriedly. We think the "that was close!" moment is over.

Soon the cop pulls him over again. Tension rises. The man left the gas station in such a hurry that he forgot to get his money in change after paying the attendant (fig. 15.1). This allows the audience to laugh and thus release tension. Once again, we think everything is resolved and the "that was close!" moment is over. Then the cop thinks about the light bulb again and walks back to check it. It's out again!

The key here is that the pivotal moment is not built around the obvious nervousness of the man, or his shifty answers. It's not his inability to hide his guilty face that will let the secret out. Ironically, these things seem to have little effect on the outcome. Instead, it's left up to the fate of this silly light bulb—the proxy suspense object—and whether it will force the policeman to open the trunk.

LESS IS MORE

Another aspect of Hitchcock's use of understatement in "One More Mile to Go" is restricting the normal rules of a movie chase. Normally, chase sequences build tension through wild adventures through geographic space, fast cutting, and squealing tires. Hitchcock instead turns a chase into a leisurely, slow, everyday confrontation.

This underplayed chase all happens within the confines of the law. The man doesn't try to run away and doesn't have to be chased. He has only broken a traffic regulation by driving at night with a broken taillight. The policeman does his due diligence to be friendly and helpful in the situation.

By confining the chase within this framework, it allows the tension to be wound up even tighter. Rather than driving wildly through geographic space, most of the tension is contained in moments when the two rivals are motionless. The act of driving is actually relief, each time the cop lets him go. Tension returns each time the cop pulls him over.

Rather than using quick cuts and montage, tension is increased in other ways.

- ◢ Close-ups of man's nervous face. We share his anxiety and knowledge of the secret. His reaction shots allow us to internalize his guilt.
- ◢ Close-ups of policeman's curious face. This is a recurring hint that maybe he will finally catch on to the secret.
- ◢ Whip pans from one face to another emphasize awkwardness.
- ◢ Suspense objects: trunk key, light bulb, crowbar, screwdriver, body, money, bloody sleeve (fig. 15.1).
- ◢ Tracking shots into the objects add narrative power.
- ◢ Detailed procedure: replacing the light bulb in real time. The more detailed we get, and the more mistakes made, the more tense it becomes.
- ◢ Proxy suspense object: the light bulb. Will it be fixed?

When finding ways to increase tension in your close-call scenarios, understatement is a great way to impose limitations and a sense of irony. When each character is tense about entirely different objects, the close-call moment becomes an entertaining dance.

SUGGESTED VIEWING

- ◢ *10 Cloverfield Lane* (2016), Dir. Dan Trachtenberg—suspense objects become character tools similar to those in video games.
- ◢ *Alfred Hitchcock Presents*, "One More Mile to Go," Season 2, Episode 28 (1957)
- ◢ *Offing David* (2008), Dir. Jeffrey Michael Bays—following a proxy suspense object.

FURTHER READING

Bays, Jeffrey 2014–17. *Hitch20*, web-series, YouTube.
Truffaut, François 1986. *Hitchcock / Truffaut with the collaboration of Helen G. Scott*, Paladin, London.

CHAPTER 16
MACGUFFIN: THE SIDE EFFECT OF SUSPENSE

FILMMAKERS AND FILM ENTHUSIASTS may be familiar with the concept of the MacGuffin. What many may not fully understood is the Mac-Guffin's role in a suspense film, and why it even exists.

There is much vagueness and misinterpretation about the definition of MacGuffin. While it is commonly described as a plot device that carries the story forward, I've realized that to Hitchcock it was even more profound than that. He must have realized early on that through his emphasis on visual storytelling, certain aspects of the plot could be minimized and even eliminated entirely without the audience caring.

It's a phenomenon unique to moving images. Film requires abbreviation in a way that is much different from other forms of storytelling. In plays and novels there are no close-ups, no reaction shots, and no visually constructed ideas. The ideas in plays and novels are constructed through words, and those words are much more vital to the story than they are in a film. Film is more like a daydream, where facts and words don't really drive the audience like they do in those other forms.

Because you've lured the audience to such a high degree of empathy for the characters through cinematic means (hands, feet, objects, personified camera, etc.), the reason behind their plight becomes less important for the viewer. Something bad is happening to them and it doesn't matter what. The only use for the MacGuffin is to serve as a pivotal reason for the story to move forward.

Think about it this way:

- ▲ Story is the vehicle.
- ▲ Characters are the passengers in the vehicle.
- ▲ MacGuffin is a new type of fuel that powers the vehicle.

The passengers are sitting in the vehicle powered by MacGuffin. They turn on the ignition and the engine works. Nobody asks why. It just works. MacGuffin can be gasoline, steam, solar power—whatever—the car moves forward and the passengers are happy. When they find out what the fuel is, the response is a short, "oh, cool," and then they move on.

The MacGuffin makes cinema different from the stage. On stage, the audience member sits in one seat and sees the same perspective through the entire play. The plot here is everything. In a movie, you shift the camera around, you show the audience details and secrets; you tease them, trick them, and surprise them. You involve the audience so strongly in the visual world you've created that the plot becomes a formality. I liken it in that way to a video game.

In other words, the MacGuffin is the side effect of doing everything that we've explored in this book. By building a story around hands, feet, objects, secrets, close calls, camera orchestration, and setting up an active game between director and audience, the very enjoyment of watching the film is not necessarily reliant on the story anymore.

To sum it up simply: The MacGuffin is a plot device, or gimmick, upon which to hang the forward momentum in a film.

It is usually an object, or an idea, or a piece of information.

- ▲ In a spy picture: the secret plans that the villains are after.
- ▲ In a murder mystery: the piece of evidence that will convict the suspect.
- ▲ In a psychological thriller: the trigger of anxiety.

Take, for example, the MacGuffin in *Torn Curtain* (1966)—a complex physics formula. While Michael and Gustav care about it, and each side will wield government powers to hide it, the viewer could care less. All we care about is that Michael and his fiancée, Sarah, escape Germany unharmed. The reason they are escaping means very little to us. It's just an excuse to build all these fun suspense scenarios.

What about the color red in *Marnie* (1963)? Every time Marnie sees red, she freaks out. Red is part of her psychological dilemma, tied to a traumatic event in childhood where she saw lots of blood. OK, great. That's not what the movie is about, though. The movie is really about her being blackmailed and getting out of a jail sentence. Whether she freaks out over red, or blue, or pink rabbits—all that matters is that she freaks out so Mark will try to "save" her.

The door key in *Dial M for Murder* (1954) is the piece of evidence that inevitably convicts Tony. Characters are moving and hiding keys all over the place, and it's a great shell game. But the real suspense is around whether Inspector Hubbard can trick Tony into slipping up and revealing his role in the murder. The key could be any object. It's just a MacGuffin.

The MacGuffin is the reason behind everything happening, but once the audience finds out, they don't really care. It's like the wild card. It's x in the algebraic formula of story. It can be anything. Change x to something else and the story stays the same.

That's not to say that story isn't important. Writers must be clever in what they present, and it should all make sense. But once you get that story framework in place, it can all be changed at any time, because the thrust of your movie is the style of presentation, not the content.

Hitchcock compared this to an artist painting a portrait of a basket of apples. Someone comes along and starts worrying about whether the apples he's painting are sweet or sour. "Who cares?" asked Hitchcock. "It's the style and manner that he's painting them—that's where the emotion comes from" (Schickel). Filmmaking is just like painting in that way, in that it's the style of screen presentation that creates the emotion.

In Part Five we explored the use of detail that can be sharpened to increase clarity and tension. In Part Six we'll step back and look at the space around the actor, and how that space and environment can be manipulated to increase suspense.

FURTHER READING

Bays, Jeffrey 2004–14. *Film Techniques of Alfred Hitchcock*, website, *Borgus.com*.

Bays, Jeffrey 2013. *How to Turn Your Boring Movie into a Hitchcock Thriller.* Borgus Productions.

Condon, Paul and Sangster, Jim 1999. *The Complete Hitchcock,* Virgin Publishing.

Gottlieb, Sidney 1997. *Hitchcock on Hitchcock: Selected Writings and Interviews*, Los Angeles.

Schickel, Richard 1973. *The Men Who Made the Movies: Hitchcock,* The American Cinematheque TV series.

PART SIX
PLAYING WITH SPACE

CHAPTER 17
LOCATIONS THAT PUSH STORY

A rule that I've always followed is: Never use a setting simply as a background . . . You've got to make the setting work dramatically. You can't just use it as a background. In other words, the locale must be functional. All backgrounds must function.—ALFRED HITCHCOCK (Gottlieb)

WHEN IT COMES TO DIRECTING, the space around an actor is equally as important as their face. Australian film scholar Adrian Martin describes the art of film as simply "bodies in space."

The sky, ground, and architecture surrounding your characters is an essential tool for increasing the feelings of tension and suspense. Whether you manipulate the environment itself to push the story, or put the camera in a place that elicits anxiety, dramatic space is vital in making your audience feel engaged in your story.

Locations are useful to suspense for three reasons:

1. To embellish an underlying mood that either coincides with—or starkly contrasts with—the scariness of the situation.
2. To push back against the characters, prevent them from reaching their goals.
3. To become an antagonist personified.

When I say "location" in this chapter, I'm referring to the environment, buildings, cars, extras, animals, and everything else contained within a space that can be summoned for dramatic purposes.

Suspense and locations share a symbiotic relationship. When you think of Hitchcock's greatest suspense scenes, you might think of museums, national monuments, windmills, trains, buses, tennis courts, movie theaters, streets filled with crowds, or even an empty field. These settings are diverse, usually in public spaces, and often in broad daylight.

Hitchcock liked to break the cliché and get away from the dark, stormy night with howling wolves that most people associate with suspense. That's why he often chose the opposite—bright sunny locations—to prove that scary things can happen during the day as well.

TO ENHANCE CLAUSTROPHOBIA

Designing the set space to be unnaturally small can help create a claustrophobic feeling. Add some oversized props and it can feel like the setting is overpowering the characters. With dolly shots tracking to one side, the parallax effect of these objects moving against the room and its inhabitants helps increase this uncomfortable feeling even further.

In Hitchcock's TV episode "Banquo's Chair" (1959), Hitchcock used props like candelabras partially intruding into the camera space to obstruct the view of the actors. This enhances the feeling of the antagonist's hidden guilt and his sense that the haunted house is pressing down on his conscience.

In Hitchcock's TV episode "Lamb to the Slaughter," the design of the set allows for long tracking shots as Mary dramatically walks through her home. As she is arguing with her husband in the living room, she turns away and walks through the kitchen and into the garage to grab a frozen leg of lamb. Then she walks all the way back through the space to hit her husband over the head with it.

Later, this long, deep set allows for some interesting compositions putting the oven (where the lamb is cooking) in the background between two detectives mid-ground, with Mary in the foreground nervously listening. And the episode finishes with a notable tracking shot into Mary's laughing face, as she gets away with her crime.

A FLAT WASTELAND

Even a flat, empty terrain can cause a claustrophobic feeling. Consider a field of dead prairie grass and corn stalks, with the afternoon sun shining bright. A straight highway and intersecting dirt road both stretch into the horizon in all directions. A small crop-duster airplane flies in the distance.

How do you create suspense in this empty environment? Find something that is part of the setting—the airplane. It begins flying over the protagonist, Thornhill (Cary Grant), and its pilot shoots bullets at him. That's the setup for the famous crop-duster scene in *North by Northwest* (1959).

To further utilize the setting, where can the protagonist hide from the pilot? He attempts to flag down passing traffic. That doesn't work. Of course not, it's a Hitchcock film—bystanders never help. He can hide within the dead corn stalks. The chess game continues as the pilot sprays the corn with poisonous pesticide, forcing Thornhill out of hiding.

Every element of suspense in this scene comes as part of the setting. Tension is increased when the setting and its inhabitants push back.

SUSPENSE IN A CROWD

Probably the most compelling reason for putting suspense out in the sunshine, aside from breaking the cliché, is to emphasize that no one helps in a crisis, not even the police. Depending on the secret being hidden, you might not want those bystanders to know. Flaunting the secret out in the open allows you to build suspense around its inevitable exposure.

When Thornhill is trapped in a public auction in *North by Northwest*, he is being pursued by the criminals in charge of the auction. They have blocked the exits with guards that would grab him if he tried to escape. No one in the crowd realizes what is going on, but Thornhill figures out an ingenious way to use their ignorance to his advantage.

How can Thornhill escape an auction? By bidding. He yells wildly overpriced bids and heckles the proceedings, causing such an uproar that he punches someone nearby. That gets him arrested by the bumbling police, and hauled away to safety, right past the guards who helplessly stare at him on his way out.

Hitchcock used the setting of the auction to function as part of the suspense. Take a look at the Triad of Secrets for the *North by Northwest* auction scene:

◢ Thornhill knows a secret.
◢ The criminals know a different secret.
◢ The crowd/police knows nothing.
◢ The viewer knows more than everyone else.

The scene plays upon feelings of embarrassment as the criminals hope their cover isn't blown. Thornhill was able to maneuver his way into police custody by embarrassing himself in front of a crowd, and still without revealing any secret. It's a complex web of threats and embarrassments that makes the scene deliciously entertaining.

SETTING DELAYS THE ACTION

The setting and its inhabitants can distract, block, or delay the protagonist and increase their feeling of anxiety. This, in turn, can increase our empathy for them. When the policeman stops Marion (Janet Leigh) in *Psycho* and begins questioning her, she gets more nervous and our empathy rises.

As mentioned in chapter 14, comedy tends to work best in these situations because if you didn't allow the viewer to laugh, the distractions could become blatantly annoying. Annoy the audience during a tense sequence and you might lose them. Laughter is a great companion to suspense—just like the enjoyment of a roller coaster. It creates a playful frustration in the audience, and forces more intense concentration on the important events in the scene.

Think of everything that could go wrong on your morning drive to work. A tire could go flat, you could face road construction, an extra-wide vehicle prevents you from using the passing lane, a train gets stuck on the tracks at the intersection, the police have set up a drug test, your engine light comes on, the truck behind you drives too close, the traffic light is broken . . . You see where I'm going with this.

Now, think of everything that could go wrong once you get to work. The coffee machine is broken, the water tank is out of water and no refills are available, the restroom is blocked off for cleaning, the snack machine doesn't take your money, your computer has to reboot to install updates, your password doesn't work . . .

Now, think of everything that could go wrong when you get home for the evening. A light bulb burns out but is too high to reach, the cat is missing, ants have invaded the cupboards, you receive a threatening letter in the mail, your phone keeps ringing but when you pick up there's no answer, your TV reception is bad, you stub your toe . . .

Now, think of everything that could go wrong once you've gone to bed and turned out the light . . .

I've probably created tension in you just by writing this. These elements are the "palette of worry" for your directing paintbrush. These are the ingredients of building tension into your movie scenes. Bringing them in to block your hero is the equivalent of pulling back a crossbow so it gets tighter and tighter.

The reason we do this in cinema is to make the important story elements of your scene stand out. The audience now cares much more about our hero's pursuit, deep down, because we have made it harder for him to succeed.

By the same token, if you want to emphasize a line of dialogue, distract the audience with a stray sound. A maid comes along, for instance, with a loud vacuum cleaner just as something important is being said. The viewer has to strain to make out what is being said, and then of course remembers it.

ANTAGONIST PERSONIFIED

Your setting may even become so powerful that it becomes a character in the story, or even the antagonist. At a ski resort in the Alps, a glacier becomes a character in Hitchcock's TV episode "The Crystal Trench" (1959). A man slips and falls into the glacier and is frozen alive. His wife waits forty years for the glacier to thaw and reveal his preserved body. Hitchcock frames the glacier in the backdrop throughout the film, reminding the audience of its looming presence over events.

In William Dickerson's *Detour* (2013), the mudslide envelopes the protagonist's car. The mud becomes the antagonist as the thing that is trapping him and slowly creeping in to suffocate him. (See Q&A with William Dickerson in chapter 23.)

Lifeboat (1944) is a film set entirely on the ocean. During tense moments, the weather boils up and becomes windy, throwing the lifeboat on the verge of capsizing. There's a key scene where the boat's occupants must amputate an injured man's leg, and the storm provides the wobbling that makes the procedure that much more tense. Later, another storm brews up right as the key secret is revealed, turning the tables and giving the antagonist all the power.

SUGGESTED VIEWING

▲ *Alfred Hitchcock Presents*, "Banquo's Chair," Season 4, Episode 29 (1959)
▲ *Alfred Hitchcock Presents*, "Lamb to the Slaughter," Season 3, Episode 28 (1958)
▲ *Lifeboat* (1944)

FURTHER READING

Bays, Jeffrey 2014–17. *Hitch20*, web-series, YouTube.

Gottlieb, Sidney 2003. *Alfred Hitchcock Interviews*, University Press Mississippi, Jackson, p.128.

Markle, Fletcher 1964. "Telescope: A Talk With Hitchcock Part I and II," Canadian Broadcasting Center.

Martin, Adrian 1992. "Mise en Scène Is Dead," *Continuum* 5:2, p. 97.

CHAPTER 18

HIGH SHOTS

IN THE AGE OF CAMERA DRONES, the popularity of shots from above has become undeniable. It's one of those cinematic tools you have at your disposal that is always at risk of being used "because it looks cool," yet is without narrative purpose.

High shots hold a lot of power. One reason is because we humans can't get those views very easily on our own. For centuries man dreamed of flying like a bird—something we weren't able to do until 1783 with the invention of the balloon. We place great value on real estate that gives us a bird's-eye view. Colonial forts were built on the top of plateaus and bluffs so an approaching enemy could be easily spotted. Ultimately, there is great emotional beauty to be had with a high shot.

On the flip side, many of us have a fear of heights. If you've ever dared to step onto the very top of a ladder, or edge too close to a cliff, you know the vertigo that can grab you. So while a high shot can achieve a sense of omnipotence, it can equally convey a sobering reality.

Overusing or misusing such a powerful camera perspective in your movie can spell the difference between an amateur and a seasoned professional with a full grasp of the visual language.

Figure 18.1. The famous composite from *The Birds*, revealing an objective view of the tragedy below. *The Birds* ©1963 Universal Pictures.

The most famous high shot by Hitchcock (fig. 18.1) is from *The Birds* (1963). It is the only shot in the film from the perspective of the birds, and is just before their big attack on Bodega Bay. In his interview with François Truffaut, Hitchcock said this shot served three purposes:

1. To convey the visual sentence: "the birds have arrived."
2. To show a map of the area.
3. To compress time between the two surrounding shots—allowing for the fire trucks to arrive between shots one and three.

Those three reasons are just for one shot in one film, and they are not the definitive reasons for all high shots. But it does open a doorway into the thought process that goes into a shot like that. Hitchcock felt it was so important that he had a matte artist paint the broad area, filmed the middle segment from a high crane, and then filmed the fire separately, compositing all the elements together. It would have taken weeks of intensive labor.

So when you look at your script, how do you know when to use one of these God's-eye views? Let's go through the major considerations.

STERILE OBJECTIVITY

As director William Dickerson explains in the *Hitch20* docu-series, a high shot conveys an objective point of view. As with any other wide shot, the high angle provides a counterbalance to a closer camera setup. Where the subjective view would focus close on character emotion and facial reaction, the objective view would be devoid of specific emotions and be more apt to provoke broad contemplation about the circumstances. But a high camera shot adds a certain menace to the feeling. "It's almost a clinical or sterile viewpoint, like a security camera," says Dickerson.

KEY MOMENT

This ability for the high shot to get the audience's attention is important at a big moment of change in the plot. When the plot shifts, the audience's perspective on the story shifts, emotions shift, and ideas shift. Shifting the camera to a new viewpoint helps the audience internalize this change on a gut level.

In *Topaz* (1969), there's a murder scene in which a man shoots a woman up close with a gun. Hitchcock cuts to a high shot as the woman slowly collapses to the floor. As she drops, her dress fans out onto the floor, resembling a puddle of blood. This perspective accentuates the moment of death of the woman and leaves us with an eerie omnipresent shock—the camera composition is just as shocking as the event itself.

HELPLESSNESS

As in the bird's-eye shot in *The Birds*, the high angle shot tends to induce a feeling of helplessness. If you want your audience to feel that the situation has become so bad and the characters have become so overwhelmed that nothing can be done, craning/droning up from close to a wider high angle can enhance that helpless feeling.

In *The Birds*, Melanie (Tippi Hedren) is sitting on a couch as the birds are chirping outside, clambering to peck through the boarded windows. Melanie feels so helpless that she falls back onto the couch; the camera flies upward, looking down on her. This uses the space above the couch for dramatic effect, as if the world is pushing down on her.

SUPERNATURAL PRESENCE

While the high shot can evoke a feeling of helplessness, or a sterile objectivity, in certain situations it can also call upon feelings of the supernatural. It's a feeling that someone's watching from beyond the grave. The stairway shot in *Psycho* (1960) is a great example of this. Is the ghost of Norman's mother watching? His other victims? God?

Hitchcock's TV episode "Banquo's Chair" (1959) is a ghost story, where the ghost of a woman shows up at dinner to haunt the man who killed her. Hitchcock uses a high shot above the dinner table at the beginning of the scene, prior to the ghost arriving. Its placement early in the story evokes an odd feeling, as if supernatural forces are observing from above. It plants the seed for the ominous feeling that increases throughout the scene. When the ghost finally does arrive, it's an emotional payoff for that supernatural setup.

NEEDLE IN HAYSTACK

The high shot also carries weight as a storytelling tool, especially if it's in motion as in the famous high shot from *Notorious* (1946). In what *Hitch20*'s William C. Martell calls a "needle-in-haystack" shot, the camera tracks in to something small hidden within a great expanse.

In *Young and Innocent* (1937), the camera starts from above, looking down on the crowd. This unique perspective immediately calls attention to itself. It's like the director saying, "Hey, here's something important coming up." The camera then cranes down into the crowd and glides toward the band playing music. The camera then continues to get closer to the drummer until it pans down to his face. It is then obvious that the man's eye is twitching—the recognizable trait in the criminal that the police are looking for. Essentially, with this single shot, Hitchcock is showing us the criminal before the characters in the scene find him. The characters know he must be in this crowd somewhere. Since we have already found him, it increases suspense as their search plays out.

With this long ballroom shot, Hitchcock wants to show us this visual sentence: "Here's a big ballroom with lots of people; none of these people know that the drummer is the killer."

SENSE OF SCALE

The famous crop-duster scene in *North by Northwest* (1959) is an example I often use in my scene tectonics courses (based on my book *Between the Scenes*). Because the scene occurs after a busied chase through a train station, the vapid, flat terrain of the Indiana farmland is an emotional relief. The scene begins with a sixty-second wide shot from above, looking down on a straight, endless highway as a bus pulls to a stop. A tiny little man gets off the little bitty bus, miniaturized by this overpowering expanse.

While this shot provides a change in pace for the audience to stop and think, catch their breath, and prepare for the big crop-duster attack forthcoming, it also establishes the emptiness from which the pending menace will appear and that there is no place to hide.

Later in the same movie, Hitchcock uses a high shot looking straight down from atop the United Nations building as Cary Grant walks down the sidewalk to a taxi. At least, we assume it is Cary Grant. He appears so small on the screen that it could be anyone. The immense scale of the building puts the tiny humans and their little cars to shame. As Matthew Stubstad says in *Hitch20*, this shot gives us the feeling that "he's going up against great odds."

FURTHER READING

Bays, Jeffrey 2014–17. *Hitch20*, web-series, YouTube.
Truffaut, François 1986. *Hitchcock / Truffaut with the collaboration of Helen G. Scott*, Paladin, London.

CHAPTER 19
BUILDING THE DANGER OFF-SCREEN

IT'S PROBABLY HAPPENED TO YOU. You're on a train, or sitting in an airport and someone nearby is having a heated conversation on their phone. You can't help but be lured into the drama. Soon you begin taking sides, making a decision on which person is the most innocent—the person sitting near you or the person on the other end. Even though you can't hear that other person, your mind conjures them up in order to fill in the blanks. A one-sided conversation becomes fully alive in your imagination (Lehrer).

GESTALT ASSAULT

This is possible in part because of the Gestalt effect. The human mind, in an effort to process the data that comes in through the senses, makes shortcuts and extrapolates missing parts for the sake of continuity (Zettl). The result is that we only need hints of an object for the mind to conjure up the whole object (fig. 19.1). This is probably a survival mechanism—when a lion is watching us from behind prairie grass, we needed only catch a glimpse of it to become fully alert and to survive.

Figure 19.1. When parts of an idea are missing, the mind fills in the gaps to provide psychological closure.

When the brain's imagination fills in the gaps, it automatically becomes more personal. We enjoy cartoons, for instance, in large part because there is so much missing information in the abstracted drawings that the mind steps into action to seek closure on missing information. Our imagination is fully engaged and taken out of passive mode.

In much the same way, suspense can be activated by leaving certain things off the screen. Hitchcock always pointed to his famous shower scene in *Psycho* (1960) to explain this, that we never actually see the knife hitting Marion Crane. The quick montage of all the various perspectives of the knife stabbing toward Marion creates within the human mind that imaginary continuity, so that we instantly believe we've seen the stabbing when we haven't. The sound effects of the knife's impact and the intense violin help sell the idea.

The lesson to pull away from this is that the less you show on screen, the more impact it will have on the audience, because it activates Gestalt.

BUILDING DANGER OVER TIME

Similarly, our enjoyment of fear through watching a movie can be heightened by withholding sight of the danger. In *Jaws* (1975), Steven Spielberg gives us hints of the danger lurking beneath the water, along with the occasional shark fin protruding into view. The absence of seeing the entire shark increases our anxiety tenfold. Jim Gillespie does something similar in *I Know What You Did Last Summer* (1997) by teasing with quick glimpses of a cloaked fisherman. Since we don't know who is under the cloak, it makes him more ominous. When Spielberg's shark and Gillespie's fisherman do fully appear on screen they are that much scarier, because they benefit from being the physical manifestations of what our mind has conjured up.

There's a key scene in *I Know What You Did Last Summer* where Helen is doing mundane tasks in her house. Gillespie frames the background behind Helen at just the right moment to show us that the cloaked fisherman walks through the front door unnoticed. As Helen continues her chores, we get another glimpse of the fisherman walking out of view at the top of the stairs, just as Helen turns and begins to walk up the stairs. Now we have full suspense, as Helen goes into her room walking into danger. Gillespie's camera cuts to shots of the dark closet, cueing us that the fisherman is hiding there. That dark closet raises the suspense as the scene plays out, with Helen completely unaware.

In Hitchcock's TV episode "Poison" (1958), we get a similar construction, in that we are not allowed to see the poisonous snake until the end of the film. Hitchcock deliberately lets the anxiety build up about this snake hiding under the sheets. The protagonist is unable to move or make a startling sound, lest it provokes the hidden snake to strike him.

Because we are not able to see the snake, we must intently watch the man's facial expressions to gauge whether he has been bitten.

Because of this unseen snake, "Poison" begins to build up doubt about whether the snake is even real. We think maybe the man has imagined this threat in his own mind. Later, Hitchcock reveals a secret to the audience—that the snake is real and shows it sliding under a pillow. Now the snake poses a real threat to the unwitting characters who now believe it's not there. Once again suspense is generated around a helpless viewer unable to warn the characters not to sit near the pillows.

For a director known for his creative murder scenes, it's not surprising that some of Hitchcock's best occur just out of view. We never see Thorwald murder his wife in *Rear Window* (1954), which adds to the ominous threat we feel when he walks into Jeffries' room.

TOO HARD TO WATCH

Ironically, television censors prevented Hitchcock from showing gratuitous violence on the TV screen. This actually made his suspense scarier for the viewer.

Hitchcock's TV episode "Revenge" includes a murder scene which is played out in apparent real time, but out of the camera's view. We watch in one continuous shot as the protagonist slowly opens the door to a hotel room, walks in, walks out of view, hits a man several times with a wrench, and then walks back out, closing the door behind him. Because this scene is contained entirely in one shot and without a music score, we feel the raw reality of the situation.

It becomes powerful because our imagination is provoked by the sounds of the attack, but we are unable to move the camera and peer around the corner to see it. Hitchcock has placed us in a helpless situation and mocks the seriousness of the scene by letting us hear the rumbled dance music from below.

While Hitchcock frequently shows raw violence in his films, there are moments where he withholds it from view for the effect of drawing out an objective judgment from the viewer. The final shot of *Frenzy* (1972) is an example of this, as the camera pans away and backs down the stairs and out of the building while the protagonist begins to enter a woman's apartment to kill her. In this moment we think, "there he goes again," and are essentially leaving the situation with a moral stamp of disapproval. He's getting away with it again and the police aren't catching him.

By the end of *Frenzy* we no longer need to see the murders, because we've already seen the first one, which is enough. The thought of them happening off-screen is much more powerful.

If there isn't a twist and the audience already clearly knows what is going to happen, it's very often a better option to show the outside of the building and let the viewers imagine the event taking place inside.

SUGGESTED VIEWING

- ◢ *Jaws* (1975), Dir. Steven Spielberg
- ◢ *Alfred Hitchcock Presents*, "Poison," Season 4, Episode 1 (1958)
- ◢ *Alfred Hitchcock Presents*, "Revenge," Season 1, Episode 1 (1955)
- ◢ *Frenzy* (1972)—final tracking shot.

FURTHER READING

Bays, Jeffrey 2014. *Between the Scenes*. Michael Wiese Productions.
Lehrer, Jonah 2010. "The Science of Eavesdropping," *Wired* (9/10/10).
Zettl, Herbert 1999. *Sight, Sound, Motion*. Wadsworth, pp.102–103.

CHAPTER 20

CHARACTERS THAT CATCH US LOOKING

LOOKING INTO THE CAMERA.

What some would consider an acting faux pas can be used with great effect in a suspense environment. When a character catches a glimpse of the audience by looking directly at the camera, it creates an unsettling moment.

Often it's one of those things editors watch out for—when an actor does it by mistake it can screw up the flow of a scene for the very fact that it takes the audience out of the story. It wakes us up. We realize, "Oh, that was weird."

When used intentionally, however, it can provide a reflexive moment where the viewer realizes that the film is acknowledging their act of watching. This can call attention to the narrative form, the film medium itself, or the very reasons we are watching the film.

CAUGHT LOOKING

An academic of film theory would explain that it's all very scopophilic, that humans crave voyeurism and that this is the very basis for the success of movies. We watch a film with the assumption that the actors on the screen aren't aware we are watching. It's as if we're secretly spying on the neighbor through a crack in the curtain. When the actor turns and acknowledges the audience, it can make us feel that we've been caught looking—an unsettling leap from the screen.

There's a stunning moment in *Shadow of a Doubt* (1943) where a dinner-table conversation is led astray by the musings of Joseph Cotten's character, Uncle Charlie. He begins a soliloquy about his hate for women as the camera dollies toward him: "greedy, petty, ugly, fat women." His niece responds defiantly, "They're alive. They're human beings!" Charlie turns directly toward us with a tepid, "Are they?"

This sudden stare into the lens prompts us for a reaction. It wakes us up from the fantasy so that we once again realize we're watching a movie. In turn we begin to think about the power of what he just said—just how crazy he is, and perhaps just how intellectually aware he is beyond the confines of the story. Has he spawned consciousness like the holodeck character Professor Moriarty in *Star Trek: The Next Generation*? It makes us uneasy, and therefore is a great tool for manipulating the anxiety of an audience.

THE NEW HIGH DEFINITION FORMAT   Figure 21.1

Michael Haneke's *Funny Games* (2007) contains a great example of characters that break the fourth wall and essentially take the viewers hostage along with the cast. Our act of watching the film is terrorized as much as the hostages in the house. One of the criminals turns to the camera and asks, "You're on their side, aren't you? So, who will you bet with?" While this would usually be a comic moment (as with the asides in *Ferris Bueller's Day Off*), it is instead an act of terror, as we are forced into *too much* realism—to watch torture and to be helpless to stop it.

SOLIDIFIES EMPATHY FOR PROTAGONIST

When we see things through a protagonist's eyes in a point-of-view sequence (see chapter 4), we see secondary characters looking at that protagonist by looking at the camera. With this shared viewpoint, the feeling of a secondary character looking directly at us makes us feel, temporarily, that we *are* in fact the protagonist. We're standing in his shoes. Automatically we are primed for empathy with his emotional struggles and intellectual logic.

In a film like *Rear Window* (1954), a glance into the camera provides a delicious moment when the criminal, Thorwald, suddenly notices the telescopic lens that Jeffries has been using to spy on him from across the courtyard. Because the film has been shot in point-of-view—we see what Jeffries sees through the lens—we feel like we've been caught looking as well. And then we share in the rising danger of the criminal's next move—to come after us.

GIVES THE CHARACTER POWER

This is true in all of the examples above—addressing the camera gives a certain cinematic power to the person looking at us, adding cinematic weight to what they do next. We instinctually assume that they are going to do something really significant soon. That's certainly true in *Rear Window*, as it sparks Thorwald to immediately make his way toward the apartment we're sitting in, raising the tension to its peak.

In Hitchcock's TV episode "Lamb to the Slaughter," Mary's husband spins around, looks at Mary, then into the camera, and says "Try and stop me." It's as if this challenge is directed to both Mary and us. We then side with Mary in order to overcome his extra fourth-wall power.

In Hitchcock's TV episode "The Case of Mr. Pelham," the psychiatrist glances and nods at the camera when he first greets Mr. Pelham in the night club. It's a moment that immediately puts us into the room. We feel that we're sitting there observing the conversation and that he is well aware that we are present.

The result of that added power of audience allegiance is that we are more likely to believe the psychiatrist's explanation of events when Pelham goes into a frenzy of paranoia. The irony that Hitchcock creates, though, is that the psychiatrist does believe him. With this added credibility, we then get carried right along with Pelham's delirium.

WHEN THE NARRATOR DOES IT

Generally, a supporting character does the lens-looking, as a way of turning the tables on the protagonist. But in many films (those of Woody Allen come to mind) the protagonist is the narrator. Rather than someone narrating the film in voice-over, the hero turns to the camera outside of diegesis and explains the story to the viewer. This is an exaggerated form of the "caught looking" phenomenon and serves as a way to build a personal rapport with the audience.

While it's used frequently in comedies, Hitchcock used this device masterfully in his television episode "Arthur" in order to—of course—rattle the viewer. The entire story is told from Arthur's narcissistic perspective. He talks to us while he kills a chicken, and then apologizes for being melodramatic. Then he reveals to us proudly that he's a murderer and that he has gotten away with it. "You've never heard of me because I never got caught," is his signature line.

Arthur pulls us along the story, turns us against his wife and against the police, as he murders her and hides the body via wood chipper. During the murder, Hitchcock's camera moves in on Arthur's face while he is choking his wife. Arthur slowly looks up at us and grins. He's so smug and proud of what he's done and loves that we got to see him do it. Creepy!

SUGGESTED VIEWING

- *Funny Games* (2007), Dir. Michael Haneke—Paul turns and talks to us during a hostage situation.
- *Alfred Hitchcock Presents*, "The Case of Mr. Pelham," Season 1, Episode 10 (1955)—The psychologist sees the camera before he sits.
- *Alfred Hitchcock Presents*, "Lamb to the Slaughter," Season 3, Episode 28 (1958)—Jack looks into the camera before Mary attacks him.
- *Rear Window* (1954)—Thorwald looks into the camera when he catches Jeffries watching him.
- *Shadow of a Doubt* (1943)—Uncle Charlie looks into the camera during a dramatic monologue.
- *Alfred Hitchcock Presents*, "Arthur," Season 5, Episode 1 (1959)—Arthur grins at the camera during a murder scene.

FURTHER READING

Bays, Jeffrey 2014–17. *Hitch20*, web-series, YouTube.

PART SEVEN
Q&A WITH FILM PRACTITIONERS

CHAPTER 21
"THE BOURNE IDENTITY" EDITOR SAAR KLEIN

SAAR KLEIN is a film editor, nominated twice for Academy Awards, first for his work on *The Thin Red Line* and again for *Almost Famous*. Saar began his career working for editor Joe Hutshing on the film *JFK* (directed by Oliver Stone). Saar also edited the action thriller *The Bourne Identity* and co-edited Terrence Malick's *The New World*. In 2008, he edited *Jumper* with director Doug Liman. Saar also directed and edited his own feature *After the Fall* in 2014.

The Bourne Identity (2002) is a modern film that captures the essence of Hitchcock's chase films featuring characters running and hiding through expanses of geographic space. Like in *North by Northwest*, a protagonist is on the run, unsure of why he's being pursued yet determined to face his antagonist. The film contained so much tension that I had to catch up with its editor, Saar Klein, to find out some of his insights. Klein's own film, *After the Fall*, demonstrates many of his editing techniques from *The Bourne Identity*.

JEFFREY: First of all, congrats on directing *After the Fall* (2014). It's a beautiful film with great moments of tension and suspense.

SAAR: Thank you. I appreciate your kind words and I hope your endorsement will encourage others to see the film.

J: Music scoring in *After the Fall* was quite minimalistic. Very often you would let the ambient sound of a location breathe and fill the dramatic space. How important is silence?

S: In film, silence is as important as sound. The lack of sound is a powerful tool to dramatize, highlight and often to immerse the viewer into the eyes of a character to experience the world as they do. In my opinion, there's an overuse of sound in recent Hollywood films. Both music and effects are pushed, creating audio fatigue for the viewer. For very practical purposes it is important to remove and simplify sound, so when you need to use it and you want it to "pop" you have the room to do so. To badly paraphrase *This Is Spinal Tap*: your amp doesn't need to be at 11. With *After the Fall* I tried to push these ideas to the next level. The intent was to place the viewer into the environment of the characters in order to create immersion.

J: How did you decide where the music goes?

S: I hate watching a dramatic scene and hearing the music start at the beginning of the emotional moment to "help it"; it doesn't help. Music placed in that manner takes me out of the moment and makes me feel manipulated. Some films try to push the music when they don't trust the drama or the humor or action. It's like oversalting a tasteless dish. It remains terrible, but now it's also salty. I feel like music can elevate and augment, but it needs to be placed on a solid foundation. So first of all, the scene needs to function without any music. I often try to start music in the "wrong" place to see what happens. It's surprising how shifting its placement can add complexity and highlight details you hadn't noticed. Ultimately it may not be the right starting point, but it can inform me where the music should start.

J: A notable sequence without music was the first time Bill Scanlon (Wes Bentley) breaks into a house. No music score until after he's finished robbing the people inside. He's driving away and you have this compelling, long, tight shot on his face. He begins to regret what he did, having a panic attack as the music swells up.

S: That refers to exactly what I mentioned before; I wanted to save the sound and music for a monumental moral crisis in Bill's life. Even though the "action" is Bill entering the house and robbing the people in it, the greater drama is when he's driving away and realizes that he'd betrayed his own moral code. The reason I refrained from any score in the house was to build tension. It may seem counterintuitive, since in horror films they always prime you with "something bad is going to happen . . ." music, but I have found that people are so used to music in these types of scenes that it creates more tension to intentionally play it dry. This is unfamiliar ground for a viewer so it puts them on edge. I used this same technique in *The Bourne Identity* when Jason Bourne (Matt Damon) first enters the Paris apartment. There is no music when you would expect it, just natural sounds: the creaking wooden floors, the street sounds permeating the apartment, water running in Marie's (Franka Potente) bath, until the fight begins.

J: The flow of *The Bourne Identity* is heavily reliant on tension and release. How much of the film's pacing was discovered in the editing room rather than in the script? Any big changes?

S: Much of *The Bourne Identity* was discovered in the editing room, which led to some reshoots, re-editing and some more reshoots. The script was always a work in progress and Doug Liman is a director that likes to discover things as he goes along. He's not scared to change things on the set or in the editing room so our approach was very loose and dynamic. This is a technique that I love since it provides the editor with the freedom to reinvent, repurpose and hopefully elevate the material.

J: As an editor, how do you keep the material fresh after you've seen it so many times? By the end of the process, how do you know what's tense and what isn't?

S: That is the greatest challenge to the editor and the director. The only trick I have is to remember how I felt about a scene or a performance the first time I saw it. I try to remember what made it work, and focus on that as everything else constantly changes. This is especially challenging in comedy; have you ever heard a joke a thousand times that still made you laugh?

J: Are you influenced by the work of Alfred Hitchcock at all?

S: I have only seen about three Hitchcock films and I feel very ashamed about that. But I assume that I have been influenced by his techniques as they have trickled down and influenced so many subsequent filmmakers. It's on my list of things to do; watch all his films. But I'm waiting for a retrospective since I'd like to see his work projected.

J: Looking back on *The Bourne Identity*, what did the process of editing the film teach you about suspense?

S: Building suspense is an intuitive process that is hard to verbalize. You have to feel your way through it and develop your own personal language rather than rely on technique or mimicry. But there is one important thing to keep in mind; the only way suspense can work is if the viewer fears for the safety of their protagonist. Meaning, that the viewer needs to care for the protagonist. An extreme stunt, camera work, or editing will amount to nothing if your viewers don't care about the fate of the character experiencing it. So in a way, so much of the hard work needs to be accomplished when the protagonist is not under duress. This dynamic is earned throughout the film when you build a character that's believable and worth caring for.

J: Thanks so much for taking the time to talk about your work.

CHAPTER 22

"10 CLOVERFIELD LANE" DIRECTOR DAN TRACHTENBERG

DAN TRACHTENBERG directed *10 Cloverfield Lane* (2016), starring John Goodman and Mary Elizabeth Winstead, for Paramount and J. J. Abrams' production company Bad Robot. He followed that up with the episode "Playtest" of the acclaimed series *Black Mirror* from Charlie Brooker. His short *Portal: No Escape* has garnered close to 20 million views online. Dan got his start in the world of commercials working with brands like Lexus, Nike and Coca Cola, and created *The Totally Rad Show* on Revision3.

Humor is an essential part of suspense in keeping the audience from getting too depressed during tragic situations. *10 Cloverfield Lane* is an endearing movie that uses humor to not only keep its audience entertained, but to increase the audience's bond with the characters. I asked director Dan Trachtenberg about the importance of humor, and about his intriguing influence from video games.

JEFFREY: First of all, congrats on the success of *10 Cloverfield Lane*. Great suspense!

DAN: Thank you!

J: My favorite moment of suspense is during the game of word association where Michelle and Emmett's secret plan almost gets out. It's played for tension and laughs—a delicate balance. How important is humor in a suspense film?

D: The first drafts of the script did not have as much humor and as we developed the script further and then eventually when we cast it, adding some laughs, some brightness was essential. Our subject matter was very dour, very intense, I wanted there to be some levity. I wanted the "ride" of the movie to be a complete one—to be *fun* and a nail biter. Laughter brings catharsis. And I think when you're laughing with characters it links you to them in a very specific way, and it makes the bad stuff that happens to them that much more sad.

J: Was the casting of John Goodman a key component of that humor?

D: Intensity and humor were the two key components that inspired the idea to cast Goodman.

J: I know you've said in interviews that you were influenced by video games. This fascinates me, because there is a whole chapter in *Suspense With a Camera* about how a suspense film is like a game between the director and audience. How did video games influence your approach to the film?

D: I wanted to make this movie feel very experiential. I took a lot of inspiration from the way third-person action games can achieve exactly what first-person action games do. And I really wanted it to feel less objective, and more subjective, something that you didn't just watch but experience. That generally manifested in longer takes, shots from behind, and a synchronicity between the math the character is doing and what the audience is thinking.

J: Michelle is constantly keeping track of objects she can collect and combine to escape—just like in a video game!

D: Totally. Like a puzzle or adventure game.

J: The business with the keys is very Hitchcockian.

D: My very first pitch to Bad Robot invoked images from *Notorious*. That sequence has always been a benchmark suspense sequence for me and was our reference point for our own "key" sequence.

J: What was your first experience watching a Hitchcock film?

D: I believe I had just entered the room when my camp or something was screening *Saboteur*, the end scene on the Statue of Liberty. The image of the guy falling really did a number on me when I was too young to see something so real.

J: I've found it common among films of high tension for their directors to reshoot once the editing begins. The rhythms of both *The Fugitive* (1993) and *The Bourne Identity* (2003) were discovered in the editing room, prompting major transformations. Did *10 Cloverfield Lane* go through any big changes once the editing started?

D: Michelle's backstory changed quite a bit. We all loved her ending so much and we tried so many different ways to "earn" it until we finally landed on her "silent" opening and heart-wrenching confession she tells Emmett through the wall.

J: Looking back on *10 Cloverfield Lane*, what did the process of directing the film teach you about suspense?

D: I think making a suspense or horror film is a unique experience. If you're making any other genre you know when it's working. But when you are *making* one of these movies, none of it is scary or suspenseful while you're shooting nor while you are editing. So you really have to trust the craft—trust the math you learned while watching others and employ it all smartly.

J: Thanks so much for taking the time to talk about your work.

D: Thank you. Can't wait to read the rest!

CHAPTER 23
"DETOUR" DIRECTOR WILLIAM DICKERSON

WILLIAM DICKERSON is an award-winning filmmaker and author. His debut feature film *Detour*, which he wrote and directed, was hailed as an "underground hit" by *The Village Voice* and an "emotional and psychological roller-coaster ride" by *The Examiner*. He self-released his metafictional satire, *The Mirror*, which opened YoFi Fest's inaugural film festival in 2013, and recently completed his third feature film, *Don't Look Back*. His first book, *No Alternative*, was declared, "a sympathetic coming-of-age story deeply embedded in '90s music" by *Kirkus Reviews*.

Detour (2013) is a perfect example of a suspense film in the vein of Hitchcock's film *Lifeboat* or TV episode "Poison," in which the protagonist is trapped and isolated throughout the duration of the story. The film opens with Jackson (Neil Hopkins) in his sunken car, completely enveloped by mud. I spoke with director William Dickerson about the choices he made at the script stage and in the editing.

JEFFREY: First of all, *Detour* is a beautifully constructed thriller.

WILLIAM: Thanks so much for the compliment, Jeffrey. It is much appreciated.

J: I love the choice to break up the time we spend underground with Jackson by cutting to flashbacks, dreams, and videos from his phone. These demarcate key portions of the narrative and give the audience periodic relief from the darkness of the car. Was the exact placement of these cutaways decided in the editing room, or early in the script?

W: What is on the screen is almost exactly what was written in the script. In early drafts, we kept all the action isolated within the car. After a few revisions, my writing partner and I ultimately felt that limiting the perspective in this fashion was too claustrophobic for the audience to experience for an hour and a half. We wanted the film to feel claustrophobic, of course, but we also didn't want to risk overwhelming viewers.

J: Was there a risk of monotony?

W: Suspense is a balancing act; it's a seesaw. If you have too much intensity, too much of the same circumstances, it does risk becoming monotonous. However, if you pepper in moments of relief, when the moments of intensity arise, those moments are more dramatic, more unpredictable, and consequently, more satisfying to the viewer. Movies are, essentially, emotional roller coaster rides. A roller coaster wouldn't be very fun to ride if there were no twists, turns or loops, now would it?

J: To older folks, maybe! You say you "almost exactly" followed the script and that's stunning to me. I find it's very difficult to imagine how a suspense sequence is going to play simply by reading the script pages. Are there any tricks to gauging this before production? Do you test the material somehow with mockups? I think there is a fear within any director that when they get to the editing room the suspense falls flat and doesn't work as intended.

W: I storyboard every single frame ahead of time. This is, of course, a very Hitchcockian thing to do. Hitchcock was famous for saying that he was bored during the productions of his movies, because he had already made the movie prior to stepping onto set. What he meant by that was that he had done all his homework: He knew the intentions of his characters, was familiar with the ins and outs of the beats, and he storyboarded each and every frame. In a way, we can only hope to be bored on a film set. That means we've done our homework and everything is going according to plan. Every beat advances the story, advances the momentum, and in a thriller, raises the stakes of the suspense. If you've broken down the script properly into its beats, and have drawn storyboards for each specific beat, it's easy to tell in pre-production if the next shot, or camera move, etc., will advance the story and increase the suspense.

J: *Detour* begins *in medias res,* throwing the audience into the midst of this tragedy without context. We see that Jackson has just been trapped in his car under a mass of dirt, but we don't know why. While you drop hints about the cause of the accident, you don't actually show it until sixty minutes into the film, as a flashback. What factors went into the decision to withhold this moment?

W: When I held test screenings for the film (which, by the way, is an extremely important thing to do for a thriller), one audience member said he didn't know whether he was underground or on Mars for the first five minutes of the film, and that terrified him. While that may have terrified him, it thrilled me to no end! I got some notes about wanting to know more about the character at the beginning of the film, but I felt it was more thrilling to start with the action, and as a result, using the mystery of the circumstances as an additional element to create suspense and generate terror.

J: What was your first experience watching a Hitchcock film?

W: I grew up watching Hitchcock films. It's almost impossible to pinpoint which of his films I saw first. The one that probably resonated with me the most, and continues to be my favorite, is *Vertigo* (1958). It really solidified the fact that no matter how much the thrills and chills take front and center in a movie, it all comes down to fully realized, flesh-and-blood characters. *Vertigo* is a character movie. It is about people who have been traumatized in the past and want to start over. It's a thrilling movie, but what we relate to is the human element, the theme—that is what is universal.

J: Did Hitchcock influence *Detour* at all?

W: Absolutely. I watched *Lifeboat* (1944) as inspiration for making the movie for two reasons: 1) It all takes place in one location, and somehow Hitchcock makes it compelling; and 2) it's a survival film. If you divide *Detour* into its two basic elements of protagonist and antagonist, it comes down to *man* vs. *mud*. Since the narrative is told through Jackson's point of view, we see his enemy the way he does: through the windows. Until the mud actually begins to physically invade the car, it is an invisible antagonist. Therefore, sound plays a crucial role in conveying the "threat" of this antagonist, an antagonist that no one watching the first half of the film can actually see. Even when you finally do see it, you're not visually aware of how much mud there is, beyond the mud you're seeing on screen. You guess there's probably a lot—it's a mud slide, after all—but you're not being given that information visually. I came up with an idea called the "Mud Monster" that would act as a sound motif throughout the film. Much like the recurring score in *Jaws* that telegraphed the appearances of the lethal great white shark, the Mud Monster—a mixture of crunching, cracking, creaking and ominous dread—would foreshadow the devastation that was threatened by our film's antagonist.

J: Manipulating audience knowledge is a vital element in building suspense. Hitchcock would say, tell the audience everything and let it play out. Others might say, keep the audience guessing and tease them slowly. I noticed in *Detour* that Jackson reveals a lot of exposition while whispering to himself, but never reveals his future plans that way. We therefore hang on to figure out what he's up to with his MacGyveresque craftsmanship. For instance, when he begins building something with the tent poles, we have to wait and watch to understand what he's building. I found myself intently watching these moments. Is that mystery intentional?

W: Yes, it is. The majority of the dialogue is meant to reveal character, not telegraph behavior. It was already a tricky thing writing a character that talks to himself throughout the story—that, in itself, requires a certain amount of suspension of disbelief—so we really restricted ourselves to writing dialogue that didn't "explain" what was going on. We wanted the audience to see Jackson's thought process as it plays out—that, in the case of *Detour*, is much more interesting!

J: Looking back on *Detour*, what did the process of directing the film teach you about suspense?

W: Suspense resides in the imagination of the viewer. In other words, the less you show, the more terrifying the implication is. If you show all your cards, there is a limit to the terror because we see it. If we merely hint at the terror, or imply the threat of the antagonist, as I did with the mud, there is no limit. It's human nature: Left to our own devices, our imaginations make everything much worse than it actually is. Good suspense should target this.

J: So if you had shown an establishing shot of the mud slide from above at the beginning, that would have dissipated all the suspense? You would have shown the Mud Monster too early?

W: I believe that's correct.

J: The very last shot of the film is the establishing shot, essentially.

W: Exactly!

J: You've done many things to make Jackson likeable as a protagonist, including his mock news report from the future and a rant against California weather. How important was humor to the sustainability of this story?

W: Humor is incredibly important for both the audience and the character. The audience needs the relief and the character needs a self-defense mechanism. There is a lot of truth to that cliché, when things are bad we don't know "whether to laugh or cry." Well, sometimes, we need to laugh, to make light of the darkness, in order to keep our heads above water. This is exactly what Jackson does. In order to think clearly, he must not sink into despair—and the way he does that is with humor, making jokes to himself, etc.

J: It reminds me of *Cast Away* where Tom Hanks is trapped on an island. Any influence?

W: Of course. That was the benchmark—how to make one guy in a car as engaging as one guy on an island. The way the filmmakers personified the volleyball, "Wilson," into a character was a wonderful device through which the main character was able to channel his thoughts and emotions. In a different, but also similar, way, we used the iPhone as Jackson's outlet through which to channel his thoughts and emotions. When the iPhone dies near the end of the film, and he's forced to leave it behind, that was a significantly difficult moment for his character—it was incredibly emotional.

J: At least in *Cast Away* there was beautiful tropical scenery! *Detour* is just full of brown, intrusive dirt.

W: Indeed. Not even Tom Hanks himself could withstand that kind of situation for more than a couple of days!

J: Lastly, I want to ask about music in your film. The score was quite effective in adding emotional depth in the opening scenes. Then it's used more sparingly as time goes on. What was your strategy for using music?

W: I think sound design and score go hand in hand. I wanted the design—the manifestation of the "Mud Monster" sound—to merge with the score. For instance, some creaks and crunches sound musical, and at times, the music transforms into creaks and crunches. I worked closely with both the sound designer and composer to merge these two worlds, and as a result, enhance and fatten up the sonic landscape. The situation in which Jackson finds himself is overwhelming, and I wanted the sound to do the heavy lifting to convey that.

J: Were there moments in the film you definitely didn't want to use music at all?

W: I did not start out limiting myself in that regard. I knew there would be a pretty wall-to-wall soundscape throughout, but I didn't know where I would have design vs. where I would have score until it was cut together.

J: At the end, the recorded song played as he decides to dig his way out—very powerful.

W: I always knew that I wanted to use *Look at Them* by Guided by Voices for the end credits. Even when writing the script. The minimalistic and repetitious chord progression and sparse lyrics are lonely and overwhelming, and you can't beat the opening line: "It's crippling never really knowing . . ."

J: Thanks so much for taking the time to talk about *Detour*.

W: The pleasure is all mine, Jeffrey. Cheers!

CHAPTER 24

"CAPTAIN PHILLIPS" DIRECTOR PAUL GREENGRASS

PAUL GREENGRASS is a British director, screenwriter, and producer. His films include three of the "Bourne" thrillers—*Bourne Supremacy, Bourne Ultimatum* and most recently *Jason Bourne*—all starring Matt Damon. He also directed *Captain Phillips*, starring Tom Hanks; *United 93*, based on the events of 9/11; the Iraq-war film *Green Zone*, also starring Matt Damon; and *Bloody Sunday*, depicting the 1972 civil rights march in Derry, Northern Ireland, in which thirteen unarmed civilians were shot dead by British soldiers. He also directed the TV films *The Murder of Stephen Lawrence, The Fix, The One That Got Away*, and *Open Fire*.

The success of the "Bourne" franchise is due in large part to Paul Greengrass, who directed three of the films. I'm always amazed by those films, in their intricate detail among the chaos, and how they're able to pull the audience along. They're so captivating that you forget you're watching a movie! I was able to ask Greengrass about his approach to shot selection, editing rhythms, and Hitchcock.

JEFFREY: Thanks so much for sharing your insights on directing suspense. Among today's directors I think you've most skillfully mastered the art of tension and release. How important are moments of calm in a thriller?

PAUL: Very important. It's like a piece of music. There need to be moments where you build, and moments where you subside. The storm and the calm. And there has to be an inner architecture to the piece that governs when you push and when you hold back.

J: Studies show that today's films are framed much closer, and the shots are on screen for a much shorter time than, say, fifty years ago…

P: Well, the birth of the Avid, the ability to manipulate a digital image rather than cut a piece of film on a bench—that's probably the key reason. Plus I'd say there's been a general fashion for distressed images, linked to the use of personal cell phones. People, especially young people, want images that feel like those they're used to making, sending and receiving of their own accord.

J: Much of your *Bourne* films involve cat and mouse chases. How much of a typical chase scene is actually detailed in the script? What's your process for putting a chase together in terms of shot selection?

P: Well, a lot of it has to be planned. The sequences are so long, so detailed, that you have to spend months planning them. But as with filming generally, there comes a time when planning gives way to the reality of shooting. And then of course you're looking for those moments, those details that just happen—they're gold dust!

J: Would you say that your work is influenced by Alfred Hitchcock? What was your first experience watching a Hitchcock film?

P: Well, I'd say there's no director alive that hasn't been influenced to some degree by Hitchcock. His mastery of suspense, his joyous command of techniques, his subtle integration of shot, performance, sound and editing is astonishing, no matter how many times you watch them. I first watched *The Birds*, then *The 39 Steps*, and then … and still love them today!

J: Hitchcock often said that suspense is heightened when the audience knows more than the characters on screen. *Captain Phillips* has great moments like this—in the opening sequence the audience knows about the pirates' plans well before Phillips (Tom Hanks) does. That makes the first attack tremendously engaging. Do you consciously calculate the audience's point of view when directing, or is it instinct?

P: Well, yes, you do. But to be honest not in a calculating way, if that makes sense. What I mean is, understanding point of view, who has it and why and what that means, is something that is inherent in film language. So you're always aware of it, and using it. But hopefully it's so part of your literacy that it becomes second nature and instinctive . . . if that makes sense.

J: Lastly, what advice do you have for first-time directors making a suspense film? If you could go back in time and give advice to the thirty-year-old Paul . . .

P: Study the masters. Always study the masters. They're the master because they invented the craft.

J: Thanks so much for taking the time to talk about your work! Much appreciated.

P: Thank you!

MAKING A LASTING IMPACT

THINK OF THAT MOVIE CAMERA you have sitting on your shelf. For such a small little box it contains so much power. Your camera has the power to move audiences, to make them laugh and sweat and go on epic adventures. All you need is a few actors, some objects, and an interesting location and you can create suspenseful content that audiences will never forget.

While many of Hitchcock's suspense techniques have trickled down through new generations of filmmakers, there's a real risk of them being lost. Even though his films still resonate today, as time goes on, I fear younger filmmakers will lose sight of the brilliant craftsmanship behind his works. They may feel an arrogant sense that it's all out of date. His ideas about suspense, humor, and camera orchestration may quietly slip into history.

You can prevent that from happening. You can teach your colleagues and mentees about everything in this book. You can incorporate these concepts into your own films, teach your own classes, write your own books, dig deeper and spread the word. As media technology advances, you can find new ways to make use of Hitchcock's time-tested techniques.

What about virtual reality? In the next several decades we'll see changes in moviegoing formats, a continued merger of gaming and cinema. Interactive holodeck-esque storytelling may become a dominant form of entertainment. Suspense techniques will be an important element in making those interactive stories gripping.

Imagine stepping into a virtual reality world. Within view is a window with a clear view of a couple arguing inside. You step toward the window, trying to make sense of the conflict. They notice you watching and start to freak out. Realizing you can be seen, you run and hide behind a bush. Another character approaches the house carrying a document. You stay behind the bush so as not to be seen. Then you notice that he has dropped an object behind him. You're enticed to pick it up. Do you give it back to him? Suddenly you're engulfed in a story of secrets that grabs you.

With directors like Dan Trachtenberg citing his strong influence from the computer-gaming world, it's clear that the audience/director game and the prominence of suspense objects in the visual narrative will become central to VR storytelling, combined with all the other Hitchcock tricks—humor, secrets, simplicity, sound design, etc. How will camera orchestration find its way into VR? The clever storyteller will figure that out.

Hitchcock's techniques are well poised to survive, regardless of the popular theatrical format of the time. It's becoming even more obvious that he was a true pioneer of the suspense craft—something that goes far beyond the flat two-dimensional screen he used. Something that will live through the ages.

Hitchcock enthusiast Joel Gunz likes to say that Hitchcock was the Shakespeare of the twentieth century. That's a bold statement. Will it be true? Will people still be talking about Hitchcock five hundred years from now? Will his films still be examined in high schools in the year 2517 along with *Romeo & Juliet*?

Here's hoping.

Thanks for reading.

BIBLIOGRAPHY

Auiler, Dan 2001. *Hitchcock's Notebooks: An Authorized and Illustrated Look Inside the Creative Mind of Alfred Hitchcock*, Harper Collins, New York.

Bays, Jeffrey 2004–14. *Film Techniques of Alfred Hitchcock*, website, *Borgus.com*.

Bays, Jeffrey 2013. *How to Turn Your Boring Movie into a Hitchcock Thriller*, Borgus Productions.

Bays, Jeffrey 2014. *Between the Scenes*, Michael Wiese Productions.

Bays, Jeffrey 2014–17. *Hitch20*, web-series, YouTube.

Bays, Jeffrey 2015. "Filmmakers: Does Story Really Matter?" *Medium.com* blog.

Belton, J 1999. "Awkward Transitions: Hitchcock's *Blackmail* and the Dynamics of Early Film Sound," *The Musical Quarterly*, Vol. 83 No. 2, pp. 227–246.

Bogdanovich, Peter 1997. *Who the Devil Made It,* Ballantine Books, New York.

Bordwell, David 2007. "This Is Your Brain on Movies, Maybe," David Bordwell's Website on Cinema, *www.davidbordwell.net*.

Cavett, Dick 1972. *The Dick Cavett Show*, ABC.

Chatman, Seymour 1978. *Story and Discourse*, Cornell University Press, New York.

Cleland, Jane 2016. *Mastering Suspense, Structure, and Plot*, F+W Media, Ohio.

Condon, Paul and Sangster, Jim 1999. *The Complete Hitchcock*, Virgin Publishing Ltd., London.

Duncan, Paul 2003. *Hitchcock: Architect of Anxiety*, Taschen, Hohen-zollernring 53, Köln.

Gottlieb, Sidney 1997. *Hitchcock on Hitchcock: Selected Writings and Inter-views*, University of California Press, Los Angeles.

Gottlieb, Sidney 2003. *Alfred Hitchcock: Interviews*, University Press of Mississippi, Jackson.

Hitchcock, Alfred 1937. "My Own Methods," *Sight and Sound*, accessed online Sept 2013: *http://www.hitchcockwiki.com*.

Kapsis, Robert 1992. *Hitchcock: The Making of a Reputation*, University of Chicago Press, Chicago.

Kuleshov, Lev 1929 (trans. 1974). *Art of Cinema*, Berkeley, University of California Press.

Lehrer, Jonah 2010. "The Science of Eavesdropping," *Wired* (9/10/10).

Leitch, Thomas 1991. *Find the Director and Other Hitchcock Games*, Uni-versity of Georgia Press, Athens.

Markle, Fletcher 1964. "Telescope: A Talk with Hitchcock Parts I and II," Canadian Broadcasting Center.

Martell, William 2013. *Hitchcock: Experiments in Terror*, First Strike Productions.

Martin, Adrian 1992. "Mise en Scène Is Dead," *Continuum* 5:2, p. 97.

McGilligan, Patrick 2003. *Alfred Hitchcock: A Life in Darkness and Light*, Harper Collins, New York.

Mogg, Ken 2003. "Banquo's Chair," *sensesofcinema.com*.

Reid, R. L. 1986. "The Psychology of the Near Miss," *Journal of Gam-bling Behaviour*, 2, pp. 32–39. University of Exeter, England.

Schickel, Richard 1973. "The Men Who Made the Movies: Hitchcock," TV series.

Seabrook, Jack 2015. "The Hitchcock Project," *Barebones* ezine.

Smith, Susan 2000. *Hitchcock: Suspense, Humour and Tone*, British Film Institute, London.

Smuts, Aaron. "The Paradox of Suspense," *The Stanford Encyclopedia of Philosophy* (Fall 2009 Edition), Edward N. Zalta (ed.), URL = *<https://plato.stanford.edu/archives/fall2009/entries/paradox-suspense/>*.

Truffaut, François 1986. *Hitchcock / Truffaut* with the collaboration of Helen G. Scott, Paladin, London.

Van der Poll 2005. *Kaapse Bibl*, Sept/Okt 2005, p. 37.

Walker, Michael 2006. *Hitchcock Motifs*, Amsterdam University Press.

Weis, E 1982. *The Silent Scream*, Associated University Presses, New Jersey.

Wheldon, Huw 1964. "Huw Wheldon Meets Alfred Hitchcock," *Monitor*, May 5, 1964.

Wulff, Hans J. & Jenzowsky, Stefan 2000. "Suspense / Tension Research of the Film," *Medienwissenschaft: Rezensionen* (13, 1, 1996, pp. 12–21).

Zettl, Herbert 1999. *Sight, Sound, Motion*. Wadsworth.

APPENDIXES

HITCHCOCK AT A GLANCE

ALFRED JOSEPH HITCHCOCK's life and career is full of surprises. I've compiled some simple factoids and points of interest for easy reference.

KNOWN FOR

- ◢ Popularizing the film term "MacGuffin" (See chapter 16)
- ◢ His Bomb Theory of audience-centric suspense (See chapter 2)
- ◢ Storyboarding every shot before production begins
- ◢ His signature silhouette drawing (See chapter 7)
- ◢ On-camera introductions to nearly 400 weekly TV episodes
- ◢ Cameo appearances in nearly all of his fifty-two films
- ◢ "Master of Suspense"—the term is likely his own creation

HIS INFLUENCES

Hitchcock was at the right time and place to have diverging influences at the very beginning of film history. While British, he worked with a German team and American team before directing his first film. He also blossomed as a director at the transition between silent and sound cinema. Among his early influences were:

- German Expressionists (Murnau, Lang, Lubitsch)
- Russian Formalists (Vertov, Kuleshov, Eisenstein, Pudovkin)
- Americans (D.W. Griffith, Charlie Chaplin)
- British stage plays
- His wife, Alma, a film editor

BIOGRAPHICAL POINTS OF INTEREST

Hitchcock's teenage experience in publicity and advertising surely paved the way for creating his own lucrative branding image that propelled his directing career.

- Born: August 13, 1899
- Age 15: First job at Henley's Telegraph Works (manufacturers and installers of telegraph cable and accessories)
- Worked in Henley's sales and publicity for 3 years
- Age 18: Moved to advertising at Henley's as graphic designer
- Paramount opens a nearby London film studio in 1919
- Age 20: First film job was title card designer for Paramount (UK)
- Title designer, set designer, 1st assistant director, and producer for 6 years
- Age 26: First film as director, *The Pleasure Garden*
- Age 27: Draws first silhouette for publicity
- Age 27: Set up public relations firm Hitchcock Baker Productions
- Age 29: Directs the first British sound film, *Blackmail*
- By age 38 he was referred to as "Alfred the Great," "England's Greatest Director," and "one of the greatest directors in motion pictures."
- Age 40: Moved to the United States after he was famous
- Age 40: Academy Award-nominated Best Director, *Rebecca*, which wins Best Picture
- Age 44: Academy Award-nominated Best Director, *Lifeboat*
- Age 45: Academy Award-nominated Best Director, *Spellbound*
- Age 54: Academy Award-nominated Best Director, *Rear Window*

▲ Age 54: Directs his only 3D movie, *Dial M For Murder*
▲ Age 56: Emmy Award-nominated Best Director, "The Case of Mr. Pelham"
▲ Age 59: Emmy Award-nominated Best Director, "Lamb to the Slaughter"
▲ Age 60: Directs his most popular movie, *Psycho*
▲ Age 60: Academy Award-nominated Best Director, *Psycho*
▲ Age 73: Golden Globe-nominated Best Director, *Frenzy*
▲ Age 76: Directed last film, *Family Plot*
▲ Age 80: Knighted by Queen Elizabeth II
▲ Death: April 29, 1980, of kidney failure

FILM PERIODS

Since his career spanned several decades it's fairly easy to demarcate his important creative periods. He directed fifty-two feature films, twenty TV episodes, and one documentary.

▲ **The "Hitchcock 9"** (1926–1929)—His nine silent films.
▲ **British Talkies** (1929–1939)—His British sound films. This is where he begins to home in on the suspense genre.
▲ **B&W Hollywood Period** (1940–1948)—His classic Hollywood movies, most with David O. Selznick.
▲ **The Golden Period** (1948–1960)—His first color films. His busiest period and full of his best works.
▲ **The "Hitch 20" TV Episodes** (1955–1962)—the twenty largely forgotten gems of TV suspense that he directed.
▲ **Post-*Psycho* Period** (1963–1976)—After peaking in popularity with his 1960 film *Psycho*, he moved away from his brand of cartoonish violence and into more stark realism.

FURTHER READING

IMDB.com

Kapsis, Robert 1992. *Hitchcock: The Making of a Reputation*, University of Chicago Press, Chicago.

McGilligan, Patrick 2003. *Alfred Hitchcock: A Life in Darkness and Light*, Harper Collins, New York.

TCM.com, Turner Classic Movies website.

Wt-henley.com, WT Henley website.

APPENDIX II

THE "HITCH 20"

WHILE HE DIRECTED more than fifty feature films, Alfred Hitchcock also directed twenty episodes of television, which we affectionately refer to as the "Hitch 20." Most are available on DVD.

- ◢ **Revenge** (1955), *Alfred Hitchcock Presents*, Season 1, Episode 1—A housewife is attacked by an intruder and suffers paranoia, leading to the husband's accidental revenge on a random person.
- ◢ **Breakdown** (1955), *Alfred Hitchcock Presents*, Season 1, Episode 7—A ruthless businessman gets into a car accident and is paralyzed. The only way to alert the paramedics that he's still alive is by tapping his finger.
- ◢ **The Case of Mr. Pelham** (1955), *Alfred Hitchcock Presents*, Season 1, Episode 10—A nervous man believes a look-alike is slowly taking over his identity, prompting him to change his own life to such a degree that nobody believes he's the real Mr. Pelham.
- ◢ **Back for Christmas** (1956), *Alfred Hitchcock Presents*, Season 1, Episode 23—A man murders his wife and buries her in the basement. He goes on vacation and all is great until he gets the bill for his wife's Christmas present—excavation for the basement wine cellar he always wanted.
- ◢ **Wet Saturday** (1956), *Alfred Hitchcock Presents*, Season 2, Episode 1—A rich family tries to cover up a murder by their crazy daughter, except she has a penchant for spilling the beans.

- **Mr. Blanchard's Secret** (1956), *Alfred Hitchcock Presents*, Season 2, Episode 13—A housewife grows paranoid about a missing neighbor and snoops around where she shouldn't.
- **One More Mile to Go** (1957), *Alfred Hitchcock Presents*, Season 2, Episode 28—A man hides his wife's body in the trunk and goes for a drive, interrupted by the nicest policeman ever.
- **The Perfect Crime** (1957), *Alfred Hitchcock Presents*, Season 3, Episode 3—A retired detective must kill to cover up the worst mistake of his career.
- **Four O'Clock** (1957), *Suspicion*, Episode 1—a man gets tied up in the basement with a bomb and hopes for rescue.
- **Lamb to the Slaughter** (1958), *Alfred Hitchcock Presents*, Season 3, Episode 28—A housewife kills her husband with a frozen leg of lamb, and then cooks it for the hungry detectives' dinner.
- **Dip in the Pool** (1958), *Alfred Hitchcock Presents*, Season 3, Episode 35—A man on a cruise is losing his bet on the ship's travel time and jumps overboard to win the bet. Unfortunately, nobody notices that he jumped.
- **Poison** (1958), *Alfred Hitchcock Presents*, Season 4, Episode 1—A man is scared of a poisonous snake in his bed, and his friend doesn't believe it's there.
- **Banquo's Chair** (1959), *Alfred Hitchcock Presents*, Season 4, Episode 29—To solve an old case, a retired detective stages a ghost haunting to elicit the suspect's confession. It doesn't go as planned.
- **Arthur** (1959), *Alfred Hitchcock Presents*, Season 5, Episode 1—A chicken farmer kills his ex-wife and hides the crime from the police by grinding the body into chicken feed.
- **The Crystal Trench** (1959), *Alfred Hitchcock Presents*, Season 5, Episode 2—A man slips in the Alps and is buried alive in a glacier. His wife waits forty years to see his preserved body emerge.
- **Incident at a Corner** (1960), *Ford Startime*—A crossing guard is accused of being a danger to children and loses his job with no evidence. He must uncover the truth.

◢ **Mrs. Bixby and the Colonel's Coat** (1960), *Alfred Hitchcock Presents*, Season 6, Episode 1—A woman is cheating on her husband and receives a mink coat from her lover. She must find a way to convince her husband it wasn't a gift.

◢ **The Horseplayer** (1961), *Alfred Hitchcock Presents*, Season 6, Episode 22—A priest must raise money to fix his church's leaky roof and falls for a gambling addict's scheme to win the money at a horse race.

◢ **Bang! You're Dead** (1961), *Alfred Hitchcock Presents*, Season 7, Episode 2—A little kid finds his uncle's revolver, partially loads it with bullets, and plays with it like a toy in public.

◢ **I Saw the Whole Thing** (1962), *The Alfred Hitchcock Hour*, Season 1, Episode 4—A man is wrongly accused of causing a fatal motorcycle accident.

In 2014 I began producing a companion series to Hitchcock's twenty TV works on YouTube, *Hitch20*, with a group of filmmakers and Hitchcock scholars. Together we examine the film techniques in each of Hitchcock's twenty television episodes. We now have nearly four hours of analysis, theories, and insights.

Included in the series is John P. Hess (*FilmmakerIQ*), William C. Martell (screenwriter for HBO/Showtime), Ron Dawson (Radio Film School), Adam Roche (*Secret History of Hollywood*), Hitchcock scholar Susan Smith, and many others.

ABOUT THE AUTHOR

©2014 Courtesy of Spike Suradi

JEFFREY MICHAEL BAYS has become known as a Hitchcock whisperer, teaching suspense classes at ScriptFest, The Writer's Store, Palm Springs ShortFest, Faultline Film Festival, and the Buffalo-Niagara Film Festival, among others. He is a contributor to *Movie-Maker Magazine*, No Film School, and Peter D. Marshall's ezine, *Director's Chair*. Bays is producer of the docu-series *Hitch20*, a four-hour examination of Hitchcock's twenty works of television, and also directed the Hitchcock homage *Offing David* in 2008.

He completed a Master of Arts in Cinema from La Trobe University in 2012, and went on to write *Between the Scenes*, the first book ever written about scene transitions. Jeffrey produced the award-winning *Not from Space* (2003) on XM Satellite Radio, which earned the prestigious Mark Time Award and the Communicator Award of Excellence.

To contact the author, email: *info@borgus.com* or go to: *www.borgus.com*

BETWEEN THE SCENES
WHAT EVERY FILM DIRECTOR, WRITER, AND EDITOR SHOULD KNOW ABOUT SCENE TRANSITIONS

JEFFREY MICHAEL BAYS

Between the Scenes delivers a fresh approach to film directing, screenwriting, and editing. Once you've planned out your scenes, this book steps in by shifting your focus to how your individual sequences and scenes connect to each other. This is an almost secret aspect of filmmaking, capable of evoking powerful emotions in your audience, that you need to understand and employ in your films.

"Between the Scenes is the 'missing link' of film directing books! Jeffrey takes us on a well researched journey to prove why scene transitions are the best kept secret of storytelling — because they help us connect our stories emotionally with the audience. If you want to be a better filmmaker, this book is a MUST read!"
— Peter D. Marshall, director, film directing coach

"As the first book to deal solely with the art of cinematic transitions, Between the Scenes encourages first-time filmmakers to think beyond scenes on a page to the cinematic conventions that bind them together."
— Greg Marcks, director, Echelon Conspiracy

"A thorough roadmap to proper, more powerful scene transitioning. An important tool for student and professional screenwriters alike."
—Rod Hamilton, producer, *Dirty Love*

"Between the Scenes breaks down how and why transitions are so important to storytelling and shows how they can be used to take a film to the next level."
—Theresa Villeneuve, Professor of Film, Citrus College

JEFFREY MICHAEL BAYS is the director of the Australian suspense movie, *Offing David*, and a film scholar with an MA in Cinema Studies from La Trobe University, Melbourne, Australia. He is also the writer and producer of XM Satellite Radio's award-winning drama *Not From Space* (2003), recently listed by Time Out magazine as among the top five most essential radio plays of all time. He is also author of *How to Turn Your Boring Movie into a Hitchcock Thriller*, and offers a Hitchcockian script consulting service.

$26.95 · 166 PAGES · ORDER #204RLS · ISBN 9781615931699

THE WRITERS' ADVANTAGE
A TOOLKIT FOR MASTERING YOUR GENRE

LAURIE SCHEER

Mastering your genre and learning practical techniques for avoiding prequels, sequels, remakes, and reboots, you'll discover fresh ideas and find a whole new storytelling environment in which to pitch your ideas — making you a leader, not a follower, of the next trends in media.

"Every page offers remarkable discoveries on the art and craft of writing. Most significantly, Laurie Scheer seems to have cracked the code on why some Hollywood films hit and others completely miss the mark."
> — Dara Marks, Hollywood's #1 rated
> script consultant

"If you're a serious writer, be it film, TV, web, or books, you must constantly take action to move your career forward. By knowing your genre inside and out you are well on your way to becoming a successful writer. Without knowledge and understanding of your genre you risk a fate of not being taken seriously. Laurie Scheer offers a comprehensive study and the tools you need to make your story appeal to the audience you are seeking. She will teach you how to make your writing marketable and profitable. Read this book before you write yours."
> — Forris Day Jr., writer/reviewer for *ScaredStiffReviews.com* and
> *Scriptmag.com*

"Without a doubt the best resource that I've come across for writing genre, regardless of medium."
> — Stefan Blitz, Forces of Geek

LAURIE SCHEER is a former vice president of programming for WE: Women's Entertainment. She has worked in development and as a producer for ABC, Viacom, Showtime, and AMC-Cablevision, and has been an instructor at numerous universities across the U.S., including UCLA and Yale. She is part of the faculty at UW-Madison's Continuing Studies Writing Department and the Director of their annual Writers' Institute.

$16.95 · 177 PAGES · ORDER #207RLS · ISBN 9781615931989

THE MYTH OF MWP

In a dark time, a light bringer came along, leading the curious and the frustrated to clarity and empowerment. It took the well-guarded secrets out of the hands of the few and made them available to all. It spread a spirit of openness and creative freedom, and built a storehouse of knowledge dedicated to the betterment of the arts.

The essence of the Michael Wiese Productions (MWP) is empowering people who have the burning desire to express themselves creatively. We help them realize their dreams by putting the tools in their hands. We demystify the sometimes secretive worlds of screenwriting, directing, acting, producing, film financing, and other media crafts.

By doing so, we hope to bring forth a realization of 'conscious media' which we define as being positively charged, emphasizing hope and affirming positive values like trust, cooperation, self-empowerment, freedom, and love. Grounded in the deep roots of myth, it aims to be healing both for those who make the art and those who encounter it. It hopes to be transformative for people, opening doors to new possibilities and pulling back veils to reveal hidden worlds.

MWP has built a storehouse of knowledge unequaled in the world, for no other publisher has so many titles on the media arts. Please visit www.mwp.com where you will find many free resources and a 25% discount on our books. Sign up and become part of the wider creative community!

Onward and upward,

Michael Wiese
Publisher/Filmmaker